Into the Midst
of the Fire

Sis Belinda,
Enjoy Women in Ministry.
God Bless,
Tiffin Callen

Into the Midst of the Fire

A Guide to Women in Ministry

Dr. Esther M. Pearson
And
Tiffini N. Callion

" . . . walking in the midst of the fire, and they have no hurt;
and the form of the fourth is like the Son of God". DAN. 3: 25 (KJV)

ISBN: Softcover   978-1-4568-4274-1
               Ebook   978-1-4568-4275-8

This book was printed in the United States of America.

To order additional copies of this book, contact:

Xlibris Corporation
1-888-795-4274
www.Xlibris.com
Orders@Xlibris.com
92343

Preface

Women in Ministry have come a long way. While growing up I heard that women were not allowed in the pulpit and presently some women are still not allowed under various circumstances. The 21st century has brought some change, but there is still a long way to go.

In today's society women are gaining acceptance and are in leadership roles in churches. They are called to minister to people just as men are and they minister in different ways. They may preach, teach, and pray in worship services.

But upon reflection, little do we realize we have had many women in our lifetime that have been called to God's service as mothers, aunts, sisters or other roles that have witnessed Jesus. These are roles of ministry that are overlooked but critical to the development of people as they search to find love and stability in life.

It is said that women are the first teachers in a child's life and I would go even further to say that women are the first demonstrators of God's love as He has placed a nurturing spirit within them. That spirit allows women to lay down their lives, deny themselves and take up their crosses to ensure others survive and thrive. Such selfless actions are at the heart of ministry, and so I believe that women are naturally called to minister to others with or without an official title.

Such was the life of Julia A. J. Foote. Her journey was not smooth. It was just the opposite as she faced one obstacle, hindrance, and burden after the other. But, she never gave up. Her story of perseverance as told in her autobiography, "A Brand Plucked from the Fire" is a lesson to all women that as circumstances get heated we must put our faith in the right place and that place is in God. God will never fail. The good thing He has started in you, He will bring to fruition. He will walk with you through heated trials and tribulations. He will be with you in the midst of the fire.

Preface by: Tiffini N. Callion

Introduction

Women in Ministry is a topic that even in the 21st century is still controversial. It is a topic whose conclusion most likely will not be settled until Jesus returns. The Bible certainly has a definitive ruling on women in ministry, but interpretations vary to a great degree dependent upon who is providing the interpretation. While the controversies continue people needing to hear a word from the Lord are being overlooked and neglected and opportunities for introduction to salvation being missed.

God spoke in Isaiah 40 stating, "who will go for me?" and the answer rang out from an unlikely source, as Isaiah spoke, "here am I send me". What a simplistic response to a great and grave responsibility. Many women are saying, "Here am I send me", but the response in many instances comes back, this is not a role for women.

Such is the case today, and such was the case over 125 years ago, when a courageous woman, Mrs. Julia A. J. Foote penned an autobiographical sketch, entitled, "A Brand Plucked from the Fire" taken from Zechariah 3:2. This scripture highlights the narrow escape that a sinner makes from eternal death as he or she professes faith in Jesus Christ. Prior to that profession the sinner is waiting to be judged unto eternal fires. But by grace through faith the sinner is rescued unto salvation.

When I reflect on women in ministry many thoughts come to mind. There are many old wives-tales and ill-advised sayings that do more harm than good. They include:

"A preaching woman and a crowing hen will both come to no good end"

"Ministry is an old boys club, no women allowed"

"Men won't follow a preaching woman, and most women won't either"

"None of the apostle's was a woman, so God did not intend for women to carry His Word"

All of these sayings are certainly cruel and even harmful to everyone that has heard them and even perpetuated them as truth. They are stereotypes that bring division rather than unity in Christ. But, these sayings continue on from the lips of both men and women. Though the times have changed, the centuries have moved forward, but the thinking is to a large degree the same.

Much can be learned from the autobiography of Mrs. Julia A. J. Foote as her life spanned from 1823-1900. She provides a wonderful narrative of history from the circa 1800's, along with a personal accounting of women's rights and struggles both pre and post slavery. Her eloquent writing style paints graphic pictures of life before and after her call to ministry. Commentary will be provided at the end of the book so that reading the Foote autobiography can take its full course of empathetic understanding before contemporary analysis is made by commentators, Pearson and Callion.

As you begin reading the story of Julia A. J. Foote, may your heart be opened to the struggles of women in ministry, their survival, and triumph in Jesus Christ.

A BRAND
PLUCKED FROM THE FIRE

AN AUTOBIOGRAPHICAL SKETCH

BY

MRS. JULIA A.J. FOOTE

*"Is not this a brand plucked out of this fire?—*ZECH. III. 2

Cleveland, Ohio.

Printed for the Author by Lauer & Yost

1886

PREFACE

I HAVE written this little book after many prayers to ascertain the will of God—having long had an impression to do it. I have a consciousness of obedience to the will of my dear Lord and Master.

My object has been to testify more extensively to the sufficiency of the blood of Jesus Christ to save from all sin. Many have not the means of purchasing large and expensive works on this important Bible theme.

Those who are fully in the truth cannot possess a prejudiced or sectarian spirit. As they hold fellowship with Christ, they cannot reject those whom he has received, nor receive those whom he rejects, but all are brought into a blessed harmony with God and each other.

The Christian who does not believe in salvation from all sin in this life, cannot have a constant, complete peace. The evil of the heart will rise up and give trouble. But let all such remember the words of Paul: "I am crucified with Christ; nevertheless, I live; yet not I, but Christ liveth in me; and the life which I now live in the flesh, I live by faith of the Son of God. who loved me, and gave himself for me." "Ask, and ye shall receive." The blood of Jesus will not only purge your conscience from the guilt of sin, and from dead works, but it will destroy the very root of sin that is in the heart, by faith, so that you may serve the living God in the beauty of holiness.

My earnest desire is that many—especially of my own race—may be led to believe and enter into rest, "For we which have believed do enter into rest"—sweet soul rest.

INTRODUCTION

The author of this sketch is well known in many parts of Ohio, and in other days was known in several States, as an Evangelist. The purity of her life and the success of her labors are acknowledged. After severe mental and spiritual conflicts, she obeyed God, in public labor for his cause, and still continues in this, although, with many, she is thereby guilty of three great crimes.

1. The first is, that of Color. For, though not now the slaves of individual men, our brethren continue to be under the bondage of society. But if there be crime in color, it lies at the door of Him who "hath made of one blood all nations of men for to dwell on all the face of the earth," and who declares himself to be "no respecter of persons." Holiness takes

the prejudice of color out of both the white and the black, and declares that "The [heart's] the standard of the man."

2. In the next place, we see the crime of Womanhood. As though any one, with heart and lips of love, may not speak forth the praises of Him who hath called us out of darkness into light! The "anointing which abideth"

unseals all lips, so that in Christ "there is neither male nor female." Praise God forever!

3. In the last place, our sister, as stated, is an Evangelist. We respect the pastoral office highly, for we know the heart of a pastor; but while the regular field-hands are reaping, pray, let Ruth glean, even if "her hap is to light on a part of the field belonging to Boaz."

> If you cannot, in the harvest,
> Garner up the richest sheaves,
> Many a grain, both ripe and golden,
> Will the careless reapers leave;
> Go and glean among the briers,
> Growing rank against the wall;
> For it may be that their shadow
> Hides the heaviest wheat of all."

Section 7

Our dear sister is not a genius. She is simply strong in common sense, and strong in the Lord. Those of us who heard her preach, last year, at Lodi, where she held the almost breathless attention of five thousand people, by the eloquence of the Holy Ghost, know well where is the hiding of her power.

This is a simple narrative of a life of incidents, many of them stirring and strange. We commend it to all; and with it, the soundness of the doctrine and exhortation with which Sister Foote enforces the sublime cause of Holiness.

THOS. K. DOTY.

Christian Harvester Office,
Cleveland, June, 1879

Section 8

CONTENTS

A BRAND

Plucked from the Fire

CHAPTER I

Birth and Parentage

I WAS born in 1828, in Schenectady, N.Y. I was my mother's fourth child. My father was born free, but was stolen, when a child, and enslaved. My mother was born a slave, in the State of New York. She had one very cruel master and mistress. This man, whom she was obliged to call master, tied her up and whipped her because she refused to submit herself to him, and reported his conduct to her mistress. After the whipping, he himself washed her quivering back with strong salt water: At the expiration of a week she was sent to change her clothing, which stuck fast to her back. Her mistress, seeing that she could not remove it, took hold of the rough tow-linen under-garment and pulled it off over

her head with a jerk, which took the skin with it, leaving her back all raw and sore.

This cruel master soon sold my mother, and she passed from one person's hands to another's, until she found a comparatively kind master and mistress in Mr. and Mrs. Cheeseman, who kept a public house.

24

My father endured many hardships in slavery, the worst of which was his constant exposure to all sorts of weather. There being no railroads at that time, all goods and merchandise were moved from place to place with teams, one of which my father drove.

My father bought himself, and then his wife and their first child, at that time an infant. That infant is now a woman, more than seventy years old, and an invalid, dependent upon the bounty of her poor relatives.

I remember hearing my parents tell what first led them to think seriously of their sinful course. One night, as they were on their way home from a dance, they came to a stream of water, which, owing to rain the night previous, had risen and carried away the log crossing. In their endeavor to ford the stream, my mother made a misstep, and came very nearly being drowned, with her babe in her arms. This nearly fatal accident made such

Section 11

an impression upon their minds that they said, "We'll go to no more dances;" and they kept their word. Soon after, they made a public profession of religion and united with the M.E. Church. They were not treated as Christian believers, but as poor lepers. They were obliged to occupy certain seats in one corner of the gallery, and dared not come down to partake of the Holy Communion until the last white communicant had left the table.

One day my mother and another colored sister waited until all the white people had, as they thought, been served, when they started for the communion table. Just as they reached the lower door, two of the poorer class of white folks arose to go to the table. At this, a mother in Israel caught hold of my mother's dress and said to her, "Don't you know better than to go to the table when white folks are there?" Ah! she did know better than to do such a thing purposely. This was one of the fruits of slavery. Although professing to love the same God, members of the same church, and expecting to find the same heaven at last, they could not partake of the Lord's Supper until the lowest of the whites had been served. Were they led by the Holy Spirit? Who shall say?' The Spirit of Truth can never be mistaken, nor can he inspire anything unholy. How

Section 12

many at the present day profess great spirituality, and even holiness, and yet are deluded by a spirit of error, which leads them to say to the poor and the colored ones among them, "Stand back a little—I am holier than thou."

My parents continued to attend to the ordinances of God as instructed, but knew little of the power of Christ to save; for their spiritual guides were as blind as those they led.

It was the custom, at that time, for all to drink freely of wine, brandy and gin. I can remember when it was customary at funerals, as well as at weddings, to pass around the decanter and glasses, and sometimes it happened that the pall-bearers could scarcely move out with the coffin. When not handed round, one after another would go to the closet and drink as much as they chose of the liquors they were sure to find there. The officiating clergyman would imbibe as freely as any one. My parents kept liquor in the house constantly, and every morning sling was made, and the children were given the bottom of the cup, where the sugar and a little of the liquor was left, on purpose for them. It is no wonder, is it, that every one of my mother's children loved the taste of liquor?

One day, when I was but five years of age, I found the blue chest, where the black bottle

Section 13

was kept, unlocked—an unusual thing. Raising the lid, I took the bottle, put it to my mouth, and drained it to the bottom. Soon after, the rest of the children becoming frightened at my actions, ran and told aunt Giney—an old colored lady living in a part of our house—who sent at once for my mother, who was away working. She came in great haste, and at once pronounced me DRUNK. And so I was—stupidly drunk. They walked with me, and blew tobacco smoke into my face, to bring me to. Sickness almost unto death followed, but my life was spared. I was like a "brand plucked from the burning."

Dear reader, have you innocent children, given you from the hand of God? Children, whose purity rouses all that is holy and good in your nature? Do not, I pray, give to these little ones of God the accursed cup which will send them down to misery and death. Listen to the voice of conscience, the woes of the drunkard, the wailing of poverty-stricken women and children, and touch not the accursed cup. From Sinai come the awful words of Jehovah, "No drunkard shall inherit the kingdom of heaven.

CHAPTER II

Religious Impressions— Learning the Alphabet

I do not remember having any distinct religious impression until I was about eight years old. At this time there was a "big meeting," as it was called, held in the church to which my parents belonged. Two of the ministers called at our house: one had long gray hair and beard, such as I had never seen before. He came to me, placed his hand on my head, and asked me if I prayed. I said, "Yes, sir," but was so frightened that I fell down on my knees before him and began to say the only prayer I knew, "Now I lay me down to sleep." He lifted me up, saying, "You must be a good girl and pray." He prayed for me long and loud. I trembled with fear, and cried as though my heart would break, for I thought he was the Lord, and I must die. After they had gone, my mother talked with me about my soul more than she ever had before, and told me that this preacher

was a good man, but not the Lord; and that, if I were a, good girl, and said my prayers, I would go to heaven. This gave me great comfort. I stopped crying, but continued to say, "Now I lay me." A white woman, who came to our house to sew, taught me the Lord's prayer. No tongue can tell the joy that filled my poor heart when I could repeat, "Our Father, which art in heaven." It has always seemed to me that I was converted at this time.

When my father had family worship, which was every Sunday morning, he used to sing,

> "Lord, in the morning thou shalt hear
> My voice ascending high."

I took great delight in this worship, and began to have a desire to learn to read the Bible. There were none of our family able to read except my father, who had picked up a little here and there, and who could, by carefully spelling out the words, read a little in the New Testament, which was a great pleasure to him. My father would very gladly have educated his children, but there were no schools where colored children were allowed. One day, when he was reading, I asked him to teach me the letters. He replied, "Child, I hardly know them myself." Nevertheless, he

Section 16

commenced with "A," and taught me the alphabet. Imagine, if you can, my childish glee over this, my first lesson. The children of the present time, taught at five years of age, can not realize my joy at being able to say the entire alphabet when I was nine years old.

I still continued to repeat the Lord's prayer and "Now I lay me," & c., but not so often as I had done months before. Perhaps I had begun to backslide, for I was but a child, surrounded by children, and deprived of the proper kind I of teaching. This is my only excuse for not proving as faithful to God as I should have done.

Dear children, with enlightened Christian parents to teach you, how thankful you should be that "from a child you are able to say that you have known the Holy Scriptures, which are able to make you wise unto salvation, through faith which is in Christ Jesus." I hope all my young readers will heed the admonition, "Remember now thy Creator in the days of thy youth," etc. It will save you from a thousand snares to mind religion young. God says: "I love those that love me, and those that seek me early shall find me." Oh! I am glad that we are never too young to pray, or too ignorant or too sinful. The younger,

Section 17

the more welcome. You have nothing to fear, dear children; come right to Jesus.

Why was Adam afraid of the voice of God in the garden? It was not a strange voice; it was a voice he had always loved. Why did he flee away, and hide himself among the trees? It was because he had disobeyed God. Sin makes us afraid of God, who is holy; nothing but sin makes us fear One so good and so kind. It is a sin for children to disobey their parents. The Bible says: "Honor thy father and thy mother." Dear children, honor your parents by loving and obeying them. If Jesus, the Lord of glory, was subject and obedient to his earthly parents, will you not try to follow" his example? Lift up your hearts to the dear, loving Jesus, who, when on earth, took little children in his arms, and blessed them. He will help you, if you pray, "Our Father, which art in heaven, thy dear Son, Jesus Christ, my Saviour, did say, "Suffer little children to come unto me.' I am a little child, and I come to thee. Draw near to me, I pray thee. Hear me, and forgive the many wicked things I have done, and accept my thanks for the many good gifts thou hast given me. Most of all, I thank thee, dear Father, for the gift of thy dear Son, Jesus Christ, who died for me, and for whose sake I pray thee hear my prayer. Amen."

CHAPTER III

The Primes—Going to School

When I was ten years of age I was sent to live in the country with a family by the name of Prime. They had no children, and soon became quite fond of me. I really think Mrs. Prime loved me. She had a brother who was dying with consumption, and she herself was a cripple. For some time after I went there, Mr. John, the brother, was able to walk from his father's house, which was quiet near, to ours, and I used to stand, with tears in my eyes, and watch him as he slowly moved across the fields, leaning against the fence to rest himself by the way. I heard them say he could not live much longer, and that worried me dreadfully; and then I used to wonder if he said his prayers. He always treated me kindly, and often stopped to talk with me.

One day, as he started for home, I stepped up to him and said, "Mr. John, do you say your prayers?" and then I began to cry. He looked at me for a moment, then took my hand

in his and said: "Sometimes I pray; do you?" I answered, "Yes, sir." Then said he, "You must pray for me"—and turned and left me. I ran to the barn, fell down on my knees, and said: "Our Father, who art in heaven, send that good man to put his hand on Mr. John's head." I repeated this many times a day as long as he lived. After his death I heard them say he died very happy, and had gone to heaven. Oh, how my little heart leaped for joy when I heard that Mr. John had gone to heaven; I was sure the good man had been there and laid his hand on his head. "Bless the Lord, O my soul, and all that is within me praise his holy name," for good men and good women, who are not afraid to teach dear children to pray.

The Primes being an old and influential family, they were able to send me to a country school, where I was well treated by both teacher and scholars.

Children were trained very differently in those days from what they are now. We were taught to treat those older than ourselves with great respect. Boys were required to make a bow, and girls to drop a courtesy, to any person whom they might chance to meet in the street. Now, many of us dread to meet children almost as much as we do the half-drunken

Section 20

men coming out of the saloons. Who is to blame for this? Parents, are you training your children in the way they should go? Are you teaching them obedience and respect? Are you bringing your little ones to Jesus? Are they found at your side in the house of God, on Sunday, or are they roving the streets or fields? Or, what is worse, are they at home reading books or newspapers that corrupt the heart, bewilder the mind, and lead down to the bottomless pit? Father, mother, look on this picture, and then on the dear children God has given you to train up for lives of usefulness that will fit them for heaven. May the dear Father reign in and rule over you, is the prayer of one who desires to meet you all in heaven.

CHAPTER IV

My Teacher hung for Crime

My great anxiety to read the Testament caused me to learn to spell quite rapidly, and I was just commencing to read when a great, calamity came upon us. Our teacher's name was John Van Paten. He was keeping company with a young lady, who repeated to him a remark made by a lady friend of hers, to the effect that John Van Paten was not very smart, and she didn't see why this young lady should wish to marry him. He became very angry, and, armed with a shotgun, proceeded to the lady's house, and shot her dead. She fell, surrounded by her five weeping children. He then started for town, to give himself up to the authorities. On the way he met the woman's husband and told him what he had done. The poor husband found, on reaching home, that John's words were but too true; his wife had died almost instantly.

After the funeral, the bereaved man went to the prison and talked with John and prayed for his conversion until his prayers were answered, and John Van Paten, the murderer, professed faith in Christ.

Finally the day came for the condemned to be publicly hung (they did not plead emotional insanity in those days). Everybody went to the execution, and I with the rest. Such a sight! Never shall I forget the execution of my first school-teacher. On the scaffold he made a speech, which I cannot remember, only that he said he was happy, and ready to die. He sang a hymn, the chorus of which was,

> "I am bound for the kingdom;
> Will you go to glory with me?"
> clasping his hands, and rejoicing all the while.

The remembrance of this scene left such an impression upon my mind that I could not sleep for many a night. As soon as I fell into a doze, I could see my teacher's head tumbling about the room as fast as it could go; I would waken with a scream, and could not be quieted until some one came and staid with me.

Never since that day have I heard of a person being hung, but a shudder runs through my whole frame, and a trembling seizes me. Oh, what a barbarous thing is the taking of human life, even though it be "a life for a

life," as many believe God commands. That was the old dispensation. Jesus said: "A new commandment I give unto you, that ye love one another." Again: "Resist not evil; but whosoever shall smite thee on thy right cheek, turn to him the other also." Living as we do in the Gospel dispensation, may God help us to follow the precepts and example of Him, who, when he was reviled, reviled not again, and in the agony of death prayed: "Father, forgive them, for they know not what they do." Christian men, vote as you pray, that the legalized traffic in ardent spirits may be abolished, and God grant that capital punishment may be banished from our land.

CHAPTER V

An Undeserved Whipping

All this time the Primes had treated me as though I were their own child. Now my feelings underwent a great change toward them; my dislike for them was greater than my love had been, and this was the reason. One day, Mrs. Prime, having company, sent me to the cellar to bring up some little pound cakes, which she had made a few days previously. There were but two or three left; these I brought to her. She asked me where the rest were. I told her "I didn't know." At this she grew very angry, and said, "I'll make you know, when the company is gone." She, who had always been so kind and motherly, frightened me so by her looks and action that I trembled so violently I could not speak. This was taken as an evidence of my guilt. The dear Lord alone knows how my little heart ached, for I was entirely innocent of the crime laid to my charge. I had no need to steal anything, for I had a plenty of everything there was.

Section 25

There was a boy working for Mr. Prime that I always thought took the cakes, for I had seen him put his hand into his pocket hastily, and wipe his mouth carefully, if he met anyone on his way from the cellar. But

37

what could I do? I could not prove it, and his stout denial was believed as against my unsupported word.

That night I wished over and over again that I could be hung as John Van Paten had been. In the darkness and silence, Satan came to me and told me to go to the barn and hang myself. In the morning I was fully determined to do so. I went to the barn for that purpose, but that boy, whom I disliked very much, was there, and he laughed at me as hard as he could. All at once my weak feelings left me, and I sprang at him in a great rage, such as I had never known before; but he eluded my grasp, and ran away, laughing. Thus was I a second time saved from a dreadful sin.

That day, Mr. and Mrs. Prime, on their return from town, brought a rawhide. This Mrs. Prime applied to my back until she was tired, all the time insisting that I should confess that I took the cakes. This, of course, I could not do. She then put the rawhide up,

Section 26

saying, "I'll use it again to-morrow; I am determined to make you tell the truth."

That afternoon Mrs. Prime went away, leaving me alone in the house. I carried the rawhide out to the wood pile, the axe, and cut it up into small pieces, which I threw away, determined not to be whipped with that thing again. The next morning I rose very early, before anyone else was up in the house, and started for home. It was a long, lonely road, through the woods; every sound frightened me, and made me run for fear someone was after me. When I reached home, I told my mother all that had happened, but she did not say very much about it. In the afternoon Mr. and Mrs. Prime came to the house, and had a long talk with us about the affair. My mother did not believe I had told a falsehood, though she did not say much before me. She told me in after years that she talked very sharply to the Primes when I was not by. They promised not to whip me again, and my mother sent me back with them, very much against my will.

They were as kind to me as ever, after my return, though I did not think so at the time. I was not contented to stay there, and left when I was about twelve years old. The experience of that last year made me quite a

Section 27

hardened sinner. I did not pray very often, and, when I did, something seemed to say to me, "That good man, with the white hair, don't like you anymore."

CHAPTER VI

Varied Experiences—
First and Last Dancing

I HAD grown to be quite a large girl by this time, so that my mother arranged for me to stay at home, do the work, and attend the younger children while she went out to days' work. My older sister went to service, and the entire care of four youngsters devolved upon me—a thing which I did not at all relish.

About this time my parents moved to Albany, where there was an African Methodist Church. My father and mother both joined the church, and went regularly to all the services, taking all the children with them. This was the first time in my life that I was able to understand, with any degree of intelligence,

Section 28

what religion was. The minister frequently visited our house, singing, praying, and talking with us all. I was very much wrought upon by these visits, and began to see such a beauty in religion that I resolved to serve God whatever might happen. But this resolution was soon broken, having been made in my own strength.

The pomps and vanities of this world began to engross my attention as they never had before. I was at just the right age to be led away by improper acquaintances. I would gain my mother's consent to visit some of the girls, and then would go off to a party, and once went to the theater, the only time I ever went in my life. My mother found this out, and punished me so severely that I never had any desire to go again. Thus I bartered the things of the kingdom for the fooleries of the world.

All this time conviction followed me, and there were times when I felt a faint desire to serve the Lord; but I had a taste of the world, and thought I could not part with its idle pleasures. The Holy Spirit seemed not to strive with me; I was apparently left to take my fill of the world and its pleasures. Yet I did not entirely forget God. I went to church, and said my prayers, though not so

Section 29

often as I had done. I thank my heavenly Father that he did not quite leave me to my own self-destruction, but followed me, sometimes embittering my pleasures and thwarting my schemes of worldly happiness, and most graciously preserving me from following the full bent of my inclination.

My parents had at this time a great deal of trouble with my eldest sister, who would run away from home and go to dances—a place forbidden to us all. Tho first time I ever attempted to dance was at a quilting, where the boys came in the evening, and brought with them an old man to fiddle. I refused several invitations, fearing my mother might come or send for me; but, as she did not, I yielded to the persuasions of the old fiddler, and went on to the floor with him, to dance.

The last time I made a public effort at dancing I seemed to feel a heavy hand upon my arm pulling me from the floor. I was so frightened that I fell; the people all crowded around me, asking what was the matter, thinking I was ill. I told them I was not sick, but that it was wrong for me to dance. Such loud, mocking laughter as greeted my answer, methinks is not often heard this side the gates of torment, and only then when they are opened to admit a false-hearted professor of

Section 30

Christianity. They called me a "little Methodist fool," and urged me to try it again. Being shamed into it, I did try it again, but I had taken only a few steps, when I was seized with a smothering sensation, and felt the same heavy grasp upon my arm, and in my ears a voice kept saying, "Repent! repent!" I immediately left the floor and sank into a seat. The company gathered around me, but not with mocking laughter as before; an invisible presence seemed to fill the place. The dance broke up—all leaving very quietly. Thus was I again "plucked as a brand from the burning."

Had I persisted in dancing, I believe God would have smitten me dead on the spot. Dear reader, do you engage in this ensnaring folly of dancing? Reflect a moment; ask yourself, What good is all this dissipation of body and mind? You are ruining your health, squandering your money, and losing all relish for spiritual things. What good does it do you? Does dancing help to make you a better Christian? Does it brighten your hopes of happiness beyond the grave? The Holy Spirit whispers to your inmost soul, to come out from among the wicked and be separate.

I am often told that the Bible does not condemn dancing—that David danced. Yes, David did dance, but he danced to express his

Section 31

pious joy to the Lord. So Miriam danced, but it was an act of worship, accompanied by a hymn of praise. Herod's daughter, who was a heathen, danced, and her dancing caused the beheading of one of God's servants. Do you find anything in these examples to countenance dancing? No, no; a thousand times, no Put away your idols, and give God the whole heart.

After the dance to which I have alluded, I spent several days and nights in an agony of prayer, asking God to have mercy on me; but the veil was still upon my heart. Soon after this, there was a large party given, to which our whole family were invited. I did not care to go, but my mother insisted that I should, saying that it would do me good, for I had been moping for several days. So I went to the party. There I laughed and sang, and engaged in all the sports of the evening, and soon my conviction for sin wore away, and foolish amusements took its place.

Mothers, you know not what you do when you urge your daughter to go to parties to make her more cheerful. You may even be causing the eternal destruction of that daughter. God help you, mothers, to do right."

CHAPTER VII

My Conversion

I WAS converted when fifteen years old. It was on a Sunday evening at a quarterly meeting. The minister preached from the text: "And they sung as it were a new song before the throne, and before the four beasts and the elders, and no man could learn that song but the hundred and forty and four thousand which were redeemed from the earth." Rev. xiv. 3.

As the minister dwelt with great force and power on the first clause of the text, I beheld my lost condition as I never had done before. Something within me kept saying, "Such a sinner as you are can never sing that new song." No tongue can tell the agony I suffered. I fell to the floor, unconscious, and was carried home. Several remained with me all night, singing and praying. I did not recognize any one, but seemed to be walking in the dark, followed by someone who kept saying, "Such a sinner as you are can never sing that new song." Every converted man and woman

Section 33

can imagine what my feelings were. I thought God was driving me on to hell. In great terror I cried: "Lord, have mercy on me, a poor sinner!" The voice which had been crying in my ears ceased at once, and a ray of light flashed across my eyes, accompanied by a sound of far distant singing; the light grew brighter and brighter, and the singing more distinct, and soon I caught the words: "This is the new song—redeemed, redeemed!" I at once sprang from the bed where I had been lying for twenty hours, without meat or drink, and commenced! singing: "Redeemed! redeemed! glory! glory!" Such joy and peace as filled my heart, when I felt that I was redeemed and could sing the new song. Thus was I wonderfully saved from eternal burning.

I hastened to take down the Bible, that I might read of the new song, and the first words that caught my eye were: "But now, thus saith the Lord that created thee, O Jacob, and he that formed thee, O Israel, fear not, for I have redeemed thee; I have called thee by thy name; thou art mine. When thou passes through the waters, I will be with thee, and through the rivers they shall not overflow thee; when thou walkest through the fire, thou shalt not be burned, neither shall the flame kindle upon thee." Isaiah xliii. 1, 2.

Section 34

My soul cried, "Glory! glory!" and I was filled with rapture too deep for words. Was I not indeed a brand plucked from the burning? I went from house to house, telling my young friends what a dear Saviour I had found, and that he had taught me the new song. Oh! how memory goes back to those childish days of innocence and joy.

Some of my friends laughed at me, and said: "We have seen you serious before, but it didn't last long." I said: "Yes, I have been serious before, but I could never sing the new song until now."

One week from the time of my conversion, Satan tempted me dreadfully, telling me I was deceived; people didn't get religion in that way, but went to the altar, and where prayed for by the minister. This seemed so very reasonable that I began to doubt if I had religion. But, in the first hour of this doubting, God sent our minister in to talk with me. I told him how I was feeling, and that I feared I was not converted. He replied: "My child, it is not the altar nor the minister that saves souls, but faith in the Lord Jesus Christ, who died for all men." Taking down the Bible, he read: "By grace are ye saved, through faith, and that not of yourselves; it is the gift of God." He asked me then if I believed my

Section 35

sins had all been forgiven, and that the Saviour loved me. I replied that I believed it with all my heart. No tongue can express the joy that came to me at that moment. There is great peace in believing. Glory to the Lamb!

CHAPTER VIII

A Desire for Knowledge—Inward Foes

I STUDIED the Bible at every spare moment, that I might be able to read it with a better understanding. I used to read at night by the light of the dying fire, after the rest of the family had gone to bed. One night I dropped the tongs, which made such a noise that my mother came to see, what was the matter. When she found that I had been in the habit of reading at night, she was very much displeased, and took the Bible away from me, and would not allow me to have it at such times any more.

Soon after this, my minister made me a present of a new Bible and Testament. Had he given me a thousand dollars, I should not

Section 36

have caved for it as I did for this Bible. I cherished it tenderly, but did not read in it at night, for I dared not disobey my mother.

I now felt the need of an education more than ever. I was a poor reader and a poor writer; but the dear Holy Spirit helped me by quickening my mental faculties. O Lord, I will praise thee, for great is thy goodness! Oh, that everything that hath a being would praise the Lord! From this time,

Satan never had power to make me doubt my conversion. Bless God! I knew in whom I believed.

For six months I had uninterrupted peace and joy in Jesus, my love. At the end of that time an accident befell me, which aroused a spirit within me such as I had not known that I possessed. One day, as I was sitting at work, my younger brother, who was playing with the other small children, accidentally hit me in the eye, causing the most intense suffering. The eye was so impaired that I lost the sight of it. I was very angry; and soon pride, impatience, and other signs of carnality, gave me a great deal of trouble. Satan said: "There! you see you never were converted." But he could not make me believe that, though I did not know the cause of these repinings within.

I went to God with my troubles, and felt relieved for a while; but they returned again

Section 37

and again. Again I went to the Lord, earnestly striving to find what was the matter. I knew what was right, and tried to do right, but when I would do good, evil was present with me. Like Gad, I was weak and feeble, having neither might, wisdom nor ability to overcome my enemies or maintain my ground without many a foil. Yet, never being entirely defeated, disabled or vanquished, I would gather fresh courage, and renew the fight. Oh, that I had then had someone to lead me into the light of full salvation!

But instead of getting light, my preacher, class-leader, and parents, told me that all Christians had these inward troubles to contend with, and were never free from them until death; that this was my work here, and I must keep fighting and that, when I died, God would give me a bright crown. What delusion! However, I believed my minister was too good and too wise not to know what was right; so I kept on struggling and fighting with this inbeing monster, hoping all the time I should soon die and be at rest—never for a moment supposing I could be cleansed from all sin, and live.

I had heard of the doctrine of Holiness, but in such a way as to give me no light, nor to beget a power in me to strive after the experience.

Section 38

How frivolous and fruitless is that preaching which describes the mere history of the work and has not the power of the Holy Ghost. My observation has shown me that there are many, ah I too many shepherds now, who live under the dreadful woe pronounced by the Lord upon the shepherds of Israel (Ezekiel xxxiv.).

CHAPTER IX

Various Hopes Blasted

The more my besetting sin troubled me, the more anxious I became for an education. I believed that, if I were educated, God could make me understand what I needed; for, in spite of what others said, it would come to me, now and then, that I needed something more than what I had, but what that something was I could not tell.

About this time Mrs. Phileos and Miss Crandall met with great indignity from a proslavery mob in Canterbury, Conn., because they dared to teach colored children to read. If they went out to walk, they were followed by a rabble of men and boys, who hooted at

them, and threw rotten eggs and other missiles at them, endangering their lives and frightening them terribly.

One scholar, with whom I was acquainted, was so frightened that she went into spasms, which resulted in a derangement from which she never recovered. We were a despised and oppressed people; we had no refuge but God. He heard our cries, saw our tears, and wonderfully delivered us.

Bless the Lord that he is "a man of war!" "I am that I am" is his name. Mr. and Mrs. Phileos and their daughter opened a school in Albany for colored children of both sexes. This was joyful news to me. I had saved a little money from my earnings, and my father promised to help me; so I started with hopes, expecting in a short time to be able to understand the Bible, and read and write well. Again was I doomed to disappointment: for some inexplicable reason, the family left the place in a few weeks after beginning the school. My poor heart sank within me. I could scarcely speak for constant weeping. That was my last schooling. Being quite a young woman, I was obliged to work, and study the Bible as best I could. The dear Holy Spirit helped me wonderfully to understand the precious Word.

Section 40

Through temptation I was brought into great distress of mind; the enemy of the souls thrust sore at me; but I was saved from falling into his snares—saved in the hour of trial from my impetuous spirit, by the angel of the Lord standing in the gap, staying me in my course.

"Oh, bless the name of Jesus! he maketh the rebel a
priest and king;
He hath bought me and taught me the new song to sing."
I continued to live in an up-and-down way for more than a year, when there came to our church an old man and his wife, who, when speaking in meeting, told of the trouble they once had had in trying to overcome

their temper, subdue their pride, etc. But they took all to Jesus, believing his blood could wash them clean and sanctify them wholly to himself; and oh! the peace, the sweet peace, they had enjoyed ever since. Their Words thrilled me through and through.

I at once understood what I needed. Though I had read in my Bible many things they told me, I had never understood what I read. I needed a Philip to teach me.

I told my parents, my minister, and my leader that I wanted to be sanctified. They told me sanctification was for the aged and persons about to die, and not for one like me.

Section 41

All they said did me no good. I had wandered in the wilderness a long time, and now that I could see a ray of the light for which I had so long sought, I could not rest day or night until I was free.

I wanted to go and visit these old people who had been sanctified, but my mother said: "No, you can't go; you are half crazy now, and these people don't know what they are talking about." To have my mother refuse my request so peremptorily made me very sorrowful for many days. Darkness came upon me, and my distress was greater than before, for, instead of following the true light, I was turned away from it.

CHAPTER X

Disobedience, but Happy Results

Finally, I did something I never had done before: I had deliberately disobeyed my mother. I visited these old saints, weeping as though my heart would break. When I grew calm, I told them all my troubles, and asked them what I must do to get rid of them. They told me that sanctification was for the young believer, as well as the old. These words were a portion in due season. After talking a long time, and they had prayed with me, I returned home, though not yet satisfied.

I remained in this condition more than a week, going many times to my secret place of prayer, which was behind the chimney in the garret of our house. None but those who have passed up this way know how wretched every moment of my life was. I thought I must die. But truly, God does make his little ones ministering angles—sending them forth on missions of love and mercy. So he sent that dear old mother in Israel to me one fine morning in May. At the sight of her my heart seemed to melt within me, so unexpected, and yet so much desired was her visit. Oh, bless the Lord for sanctified men and women!

There was no one at home except the younger children, so our coming together was uninterrupted. She read and explained many passages of Scripture to me, such as, John xvii; 1 Thess. iv. 3; v. 23; 1 Cor. vi. 9-12; Heb. ii. 11; and many others—carefully marking them in my Bible. All this had been as a sealed book to me until now. Glory to Jesus! the seals were broken and light began to shine upon the blessed Word of God as I had never seen it before.

The second day after that pilgrim's visit, while waiting on the Lord, my large desire was granted, through faith in my precious Saviour. The glory of God seemed almost to prostrate me to the floor. There was, indeed, a weight of glory resting upon me. I sang with all my heart.

"This is the was I long have sought,
And mourned because I found it not."

Glory to the Father! glory to the Son! and glory to the Holy Ghost! who hath plucked me as a brand from the burning, and sealed. me unto eternal life. I no longer hoped for glory, but I had the full assurance of it. Praise

the Lord for Paul-like faith! "I am crucified with Christ: nevertheless, I live; yet not I, but Christ liveth in me." This, my constant prayer, was answered, that I might be strengthened with might by his Spirit; in the inner man; that being rooted and grounded in love, I might be able to comprehend with all saints what is the length, and breadth, and heighth, and depth, and to know the love of Christ which passeth knowledge, and be filled with all the fullness of God.

I had been afraid to tell my mother I was praying for sanctification, but when the "old man" was cast out of my heart, and perfect love took possession, I lost all fear. I went straight to my mother and told her I was sanctified. She was astonished, and called my father and told him what I had said. He was amazed as well, but said not a word. I at once began to read to them out of my Bible, and to many others, thinking, in nay simplicity, that they would believe and receive the same blessing at once. To the glory of God, some did believe and were saved, but many were too wise to be taught by a, child—too good to be made better.

From this time, many, who had been my warmest friends, and seemed to think me a Christian, turned against me, saying I did not

Section 45

know what I was talking about—that there was no such thing as sanctification and holiness in this life—and that the devil had deluded me into self-righteousness. Many of them fought holiness with more zeal and vigor than they did sin. Amid all this, I had that sweet peace that passeth all understanding springing up within my soul like a perennial foundation—glory to the precious blood of Jesus!

"The King of heaven and earth
Deigns to dwell with mortals here."

CHAPTER XI

A Religion as Old as the Bible

The pastor of our church visited me one day, to talk about my "new religion," as he called it. I took my Bible and read many of my choice passage's to him, such as—Come and hear, all ye that fear God, and I will declare what he hath done for my soul." (Psa. lxvi. 16) "Blessed is he whose transgression is forgiven, whose sin is covered. (Psa. xxxii.1.) While reading this verse, my whole being was so filled with the glory of God that I exclaimed: "Glory to Jesus! he has freed me from the guilt of sin, and sin hath no longer dominion over me; Christ makes me holy as well as happy."

I also read these words from Ezekiel xxxvi.: "Then will I sprinkle clean water upon you, and ye shall be clean; from your filthiness and from all your idols will I cleanse you; a new heart also will I give you, and a new spirit will I put within you, and I will take away

the stony heart out of your flesh, and I will give you a heart of mesh. And I will put nay Spirit within you, and cause you to walk in my statute, and ye shall keep my judgments, and do them."

I stopped reading, and asked the preacher to explain these last verses to me. He replied: "They are all well enough; but you must I, remember that you are too young to read and dictate to persons older than yourself, and many in the church are dissatisfied with the way you are talking and acting." As he answered me, the Lord spoke to my heart and glory filled my soul. I said: "My dear minister, I wish they would all go to Jesus, in prayer and faith, and he will teach them as he has taught me." As the minister left me, I involuntarily burst forth into praises:

"My soul is full of glory inspiring my tongue,
Could I meet with angels I would sing them a song."

Though my gifts were but small, I could not be shaken by what man might think or say.

I continued day by day, month after month, to walk in the light as He is in the light, having fellowship with the Trinity and those aged saints. The blood of Jesus Christ cleansed me from all sin, and enabled me to rejoice in persecution.

Section 48

Bless the Lord, O my soul, for this wonderful salvation, that snatched me as a brand from the burning, even me, a poor, ignorant girl!

And will he not do for all what he did for me? Yes, yes; God is no respecter of persons. Jesus' blood will wash away all your sin and make you whiter than snow.

CHAPTER XII

My Marriage

Soon after my conversion, a young man, who had accompanied me to places of amusement, and for whom I had formed quite an attachment, professed faith in Christ and united with the same church to which I belonged. A few months after, he made me on offer of marriage. I struggled not a little to banish the thought from my mind, chiefly because he was not sanctified. But my feelings were so strongly enlisted that I felt pure he would someday be my husband. I read to him and talked to him on the subject of a cleansed heart. He assented to all my argument,

Section 49

saying he believed and would seek for it.

The few weeks that he remained with us I labored hard with him for his deliverance, but he left us to go to Boston, Mass. We corresponded regularly, he telling me of his religious enjoyment, but that he did not hear anything about sanctification. Great was my anxiety lest the devil should steal away the good seed out of his heart. The Lord, and he only, knows how many times I besought him to let the clear light of holiness shine into that man's heart. Through all this my mind was stayed upon God; I rested in the will of the Lord.

One night, about a month after his departure, I could not sleep, the tempter being unusually busy with me. Rising, I prostrated myself before the Lord. While thus upon my face, these words of God came to me: "For we have not an high priest which cannot be touched with the feeling of our infirmities; but in all points was tempted like as we are, yet without sin." (Heb. iv. 15.) I at once rose up, thanking God for his precious words: I took my Bible and read them over and over again; also the eighteenth verse of the second chapter of Hebrews. I was not conscious of having committed sin, and I cried out: "Leave

Section 50

me, Satan; I am the Lord's." At that the tempter left, and I surrendered myself and all my interests into the hands of God. Glory to his holy name! "For it pleased the Father that in him should all fullness dwell," and of his fullness have I received, and grace for grace.

"Praise God from whom all blessings flow,
Praise him all creatures here below,"

The day following this night of temptation was one of the great peace—peace flowing as a river, even to overflowing its banks, and such glory of the Lord appeared as to almost deprive me of bodily powers. I forgot all toil and care.

This was just a year after my heart was emptied of sin. Through faith I received the Saviour, and in the same have continued ever Since and proved him able to kept from sin. Bless God! all my desires are satisfied in him. He is indeed my reconciled God, the, Christ Jesus whose precious blood is all my righteousness.

"Nought of good that I have done,
Nothing but the blood of Jesus."

Glory to the blood that hath bought me! glory to the blood that hath cleansed me! glory to the blood that keeps me clean!—me, a brand plucked from the fire.

Section 51

George returned in about a year to claim me as his bride. He still gave evidence of being a Christian, but had not been cleansed from the carnal mind. I still continued to pray for his sanctification, and desired that it should take place before our union, but I was so much attached to him that I could not resist his pleadings; so, at the appointed time, we were married, in the church, in the presence of a large number of people, many of whom followed us to my father's house to offer their congratulations.

We staid at home but one day after the ceremony. This day I spent in preparing for our departure and in taking leave of my friends. Tenderly as I loved my parents, much loved the church, yet I found myself quite willing to leave them all in the divine appointment.

The day following, accompanied by several friends, we started for Boston, in an old fashioned stage-coach, there being no railroads at that time. As I rode along I admired the goodness of God, and my heart overflowed with gratitude to him, who had blessed me with power to choose his will and make me able to say with truth, "I gladly forsake all to follow thee." Once, the thought of leaving my father's

Section 52

house, to go among strangers, would have been terrible, but now I rejoiced in being so favored as to be called to make this little sacrifice, and evince my love to him who saith "He that loveth father or mother more than me is not worthy of me."

CHAPTER XIII

Removal of Baston—
The Work of Full Salvation

On our arrival in Boston, after long, weary some journey, we went at once to the houses of Mrs. Burrows, where my husband had made arrangements for me to board while he was away at work during the week. He worked in Chelsea, and could not come to look after my welfare but once a week. The boarders in this house were mostly gentleman, nearly all of whom were out of Christ. Mrs. Burrows was a church-member, but knew nothing of the full joys of salvation.

I went to church the first Sabbath I was there, remained at class-meeting, gave my letter

Section 53

of membership to the minister, and was received into the church. In giving my first testimony, I told of my through and happy conversion, and of my sanctification as a second, distinct work of the Holy Ghost.

After class-meeting, a good many came to me, asking questions about sanctification; others stood off in groups, talking, while a few followed me to my boarding-house. They all seemed very much excited over what I had told them. I began to see that it was not the voice of man that had bidden me go out from the land of my nativity and from my kindred, but the voice of my dear Lord I was completely prepared for all that followed, knowing that "All things to work together for good to them that love God." Change of people, places and circumstances. Weighed nothing with me, for I had a safe abiding place with my Father. Some people had been to me in such an unchristianlike spirit that I had spoken to and about them in rather an incautious manner. I now more and more saw the great need of ordering all my words as in the immediate presence of God, that I might be able to maintain that purity of lips and life which the Gospel required. God is holy, and if I would enjoy constant communion with him I must guard every avenue of my soul, and watch

Section 54

every thought of my heart and word of my tongue, that I may be blameless before him in love. The Lord help me evermore to be upon my guard, and having done all, to stand. Amen and amen.

In a few months my husband rented a house just across the road from my boarding-house, and I went to housekeeping. "Mam" Riley, a most excellent Christian, became as a mother to me in this strange land, far from my own dear mother. Bless the Lord! He supplied all my needs. "Mam" Riley had two grown daughters, one about my own age, married, who had two children. They were dear Christian women, and like sisters to me. The mother thought she once enjoyed the blessing of heart purity, but the girls had not heard of such a thing as being sanctified and permitted to live. The elder girl, who was a consumptive and in delicate health, soon became deeply interested in the subject. She began to hunger and thirst after righteousness, and did not rest until she was washed and made clean in the blood of Jesus. Her clear, definite testimony had a great effect upon the church, as her family was one of the first in point of wealth and standing in the community.

God wonderfully honored the faith of this young saint in her ceaseless labor for others.

Section 55

We attended meetings and visited from house to house, together, almost constantly, when she was able to go out. Glory to God !the church became much aroused; some plunged into the ocean of perfect love, and came forth testifying to the power of the blood. Others disbelieved and ridiculed this "foolish doctrine," as they called it, saying it was just as impossible to live without committing sin as it was to live without eating, and brought disjointed passages of Scripture to bear them out.

CHAPTER XIV

Early Fruit Gathered Home

After I went to Boston I was much drawn out in prayer for the sanctification of believers. Notwithstanding the enemy labored by various means to hinder the work of grace, yet the Lord wrought a wonderful change in many.

The mother of my friend received a fresh baptism, and came back into the light, praising the Lord. That the Holy Spirit might keep my dear "Mam" Riley pure until death, was my prayer.

The health of my dear friend, Mrs. Simpson, began rapidly to fail. One morning, in reply to my question as to her health, she said: "Dear sister, I have been in great pain through the night, but you know Jesus said, 'I will never leave thee nor forsake thee.' Praise God, who has been with me in great mercy through the darkness of the night." I remained with her following night, and such calmness, patience and resignation through suffering, I never had witnesser. Toward morning she was more easy, and asked for her husband.

When he came, she embraced him, repeated passages of Scripture to him, and exhorted him, as she had many times before, to receive I God in all his fullness.

There, in that death-chamber, in the stillness of night, we prayed for that pious and exemplary man, that he might present his body a living sacrifice. He was deeply moved upon by the Holy Spirit, so that he cried aloud for deliverance; but almost on the instant began to doubt, and left the room. His wife requested me to read and talk to her about Jesus, which I did, and she was filled with heavenly joy and shouted aloud: "Oh, the blood, the precious blood of Jesus cleanses me now!"

Her mother, who was sleeping in an adjoining room, was awakened by the noise and came in, saying, as she did so: "This room is filled with the glory of God. Hallelujah! Amen."

As the morning dawned, Mrs. Simpson sank into a quiet slumber, which lasted several hours. She awoke singing:

> "How happy are they who their Saviour obey,
> And have laid up their treasure above."

She was comparatively free from pain for several days, though very weak. She talked to all who came to see her of salvation free and

full. Her last morning on the earth came. She was peaceful and serene, with a heavenly smile upon her countenance. She asked me to pray, which

I did with streaming eyes and quivering voice. She then asked led us to sing the hymn,

"Oh, for a thousand tongues to sing
my great Redeemer's praise."

She sang with us in a much stronger voice than she had used for many days. As we sang the last verse, She raised herself up in the bed, clapped her hands and cried: "He sets the Prisoner free! Glory! glory! I am free! They have come for me!" She pointed toward the east. Her mother asked her who had come.

She said: "Don't you see the chariot and horses? Glory! glory to the blood!"

She dropped back upon her pillow, and was gone. She had stepped aboard the chariot, which we could not see, but we felt the fire.

While many in the room were weeping, her mother shed not a tear, but shouted, "Glory to God I" Then, with her own hands, she assisted in arranging and preparing the remains for burial. Thus did another sanctified saint enter into eternal life. Though her period of sanctification was short, it was full of precious fruit.

CHAPTER XV

New and Unpleasant Revelations

My Husband had always treated the subject of heart purity with favor, but now he began to speak against it. He said I was getting more crazy every day, and getting others in the same way, and that if I did not stop he would send me back home or to the crazy house. I questioned him closely respecting the state of his mind, feeling that he had been prejudiced. I did not I did not attempt to contend with him on the danger and fallacy of his notions, but simply asked what his state of grace was, if God should require his soul of him then He gave me no answer until I insisted upon one. Then he said: "Julia, I don't think I can ever believe myself as holy as you think you are."

I then urged him to believe in Christ's holiness, if he had no faith in the power of the blood of Christ to cleanse from all sin. He

that bath this hope purifies himself as God is pure. We knelt in prayer together, my husband leading, and he seemed much affected while praying. To me it was A precious season, though there was an indescribable something between us—something dark and high. As I looked at it, these words of the poet came to me.

"God moves in a mysterious way,
His wonders to perform."

From that time I never beheld my husband's face clear and distinct, as before, the dark shadow being ever present. This caused me not a little anxiety and many prayers. 'Soon after, he accepted an offer to go to sea for six months, leaving me to draw half of his wages. To this arrangement I reluctantly consented, fully realizing how lonely I should be among strangers. Had it not been for dear "Mam" Riley, I could hardly have endured it. Her precept and example taught me to lean more heavily on Christ for support. God gave me these precious words: "Be careful for nothing, but in everything, by prayer and supplication, with thanksgiving, let your requests be made known unto God." Truly, God is the great Arbiter of all events, and "because he lives, I shall live also."

Section 61

The day my husband went on Ship-board was one of close trial and great inward conflicts. It was difficult for me to mark the exact line between disapprobation and Christian forbearance and patient love. How I longed for wisdom to meet everything in a spirit of meekness and fear, that I might not be surprised into evil or hindered from improving all things to the glory of God.

While under this apparent cloud, I took the Bible to my closet, asking Divine aid. As I opened the book, my eyes fell on these words: "For thy

Maker is thine husband." I then read the fifty-fourth chapter of Isaiah over and over again. It seemed to me that I had never seen it before. I went forth glorifying God.

CHAPTER XVI

A Long-Lost Brother Found

Having no children, I had a good deal of leisure after my husband's departure, so I visited many of the poor and forsaken ones, reading and talking to them of Jesus, the Saviour. One day I was directed by the Spirit to visit he Marine Hospital. In passing through one of the wards I heard myself called by my maiden name. Going to the cot from whence the voice came, I beheld what seemed to me a human skeleton. As I looked I began to see our family likeness, and recognized my eldest brother, who left home many years before, when I was quite young. Not hearing from him, we had mourned him as dead. With a feeble voice, he told me of his roving and seafaring life; "and now, sister," he said, "I am dying."

I asked him if he was willing to die—if he was ready to stand before God. "No, oh, no!" he said. I entreated him to pray. He shook

his head, saying, "I can't pray; my heart is too hard, and my mind dark and bewildered," and then cried out, in the agony of his soul, "Oh, that dreadful, burning hell! how can I escape it?"

I urged him to pray, and to believe that Jesus died for all. I prayed for him, and staid with him as much as possible. One morning, when I went to see him, I was shown his lifeless remains in the dead-house. This was indeed, a solemn time for me.

I had very little hope in my brother's death. But there is an High Priest who ever liveth to make intercession for all, and I trust that he prevailed. The Lord is the Judge of all the earth, and all souls are in his hands, and he will in no wise clear the guilty, though merciful and wise. Willful unbelief is a crying sin, and will not be passed by without punishment. God judges righteously, and is the avenger of all sin. Justice is meted out to all, either here or in eternity. Praise the Lord! My whole soul joins in saying, Praise the Lord!

God, in great mercy, returned my husband to me in safety, for which I bowed in great thankfulness. George told me that the ship was a poor place to serve the Lord, and that the most he heard was oaths. He said that

Section 64

sometimes he would slip away and pray, and that, upon one occasion, the captain came upon him unawares, and called him "a fool," and told him to get up and go to work. Notwithstanding all this, my husband shipped for a second voyage. Praise the Lord! he saved me from a painful feeling at parting. With joy could I say, "Thou everywhere-present God! thy will be done."

During the year I had been from home, letters from my parents and friends had come to me quite often, filling me with gladness and thanksgiving for the many blessings and, cheering words they contained. But now a, letter came bringing the intelligence that my family were about to move to Silver Lake, which was much farther from me. I tremblingly went to my heavenly Father, who gave me grace and strength at once.

CHAPTER XVII

My Call to Preach the Gospel

FOR months I had been moved upon to exhort and pray with the people, in my visits from house to house; and in meetings my whole soul seemed drawn out for the salvation of souls. The love of Christ in me was not limited. Some of my mistaken friends said I was too forward, but a desire to work for the Master, and to promote the glory of his kingdom in the salvation of souls, was food to my poor soul.

When called of God, on a particular occasion, to a definite work, I said, "No, Lord, not me." Day by day I was more impressed that God would have and work in his vineyard. I thought it could not be that I was called to preach—I, so weak and ignorant. Still, I knew all things were possible with God, even the confounding the wise by the foolish things of this earth. Yet in me there was a shrinking.

Section 66

I took all my doubts and fears to the Lord in prayer, when, what seemed to be an angel, made his appearance. In his hand was a scroll, on which were these words: "Thee have I chosen to preach my Gospel without delay."

The moment my eyes saw it, it appeared to be printed on my heart. The angel was gone in an instant, and I, in agony, cried out, "Lord, I cannot do it!" It was eleven o'clock in the morning, yet everything grew dark as night. The darkness was so great that I feared to stir.

At last "Mam" Riley entered. As she did so, the room grew lighter, and I arose from my knees. My heart was so heavy I scarce could speak. Dear "Mam" Riley saw my distress, and soon left me.

From that day my appetite failed me and sleep fled from my eyes. I seemed as one tormented. I prayed, but felt no better. I belonged to a band of sisters whom I loved dearly, and to them I partially opened, my mind. One of them seemed to understand my case at once, and advised me to do as God had bid me, or I would never be happy here or hereafter. But it seemed to hard—could not give up and obey.

One night, as I lay weeping and beseeching the dear Lord to remove this burden from me,

Section 67

there appeared the same angel that came to me before, and on his breast were these words: "You are lost unless you obey God's righteous commands." I saw the writing, and that was enough, I covered my head and awoke my husband, who had returned a few days before. He asked me why I trembled so, but I had not power to answer him. I remained in that condition until morning, when I tried to arise and go about my usual duties, but was too ill. Then my husband called a physician, who prescribed medicine, but it did me no good.

I had always been opposed to the preaching of women, and had spoken against it, though, I acknowledge, without foundation. This rose before me like a mountain, and when I thought of the difficulties they had to encounter, both from professors and non-professors, I shrank back and cried, "Lord, I cannot go!"

The trouble my heavenly Father has had to keep me out of the fire that is never quenched, he alone, knoweth. My husband and friends said I would die or go crazy if something favorable did not take place soon. I expected to die and be lost, knowing I had been enlightened and had tasted the heavenly gift. I read again and again the sixth chapter of Hebrews.

CHAPTER XVIII

Heavenly Disitations Again

NEARLY two months from the time I first saw the angel, I said that I would do anything or go anywhere for God, if it were made plain to me. He took me at my word, and sent the angel again with this message: "You have I chosen to go in my name and warn the people of their sins." I bowed my head and said, "I will go, Lord."

That moment I felt a joy and peace I had not known for months. But strange as it may appear, it is not the less true, that, ere one hour had passed, I began to reason thus: "I am elected to preach the Gospel without the requisite qualifications, and, besides, my parents and friends will forsake me and turn against me; and I regret that I made a promise." At that instant all the joy and peace I had felt left me, and I thought I was standing on the brink of hell, and heard the devil say: "Let her go! let her go! I will catch her." Reader,

can you imagine how I felt? If you were ever snatched from the mouth of hell, you can, in part, realize my feelings.

I continued in this state for some time, when, on a Sabbath evening—ah! that memorable Sabbath evening—while engaged in fervent prayer, the same supernatural presence came to me once more and took me by the hand. At that moment I became lost to everything of this world. The angel led me to a place where there was a, large tree, the branches of which seemed to extend either way beyond sight. Beneath it sat, as I thought, God and Father, the Son, and the Holy Spirit, besides many others, whom I thought were angels. I was led before them: they looked me over from head to foot, but said nothing. Finally, the Father said to me: "Before these people make your choice, whether you will obey me or go from this place to eternal misery and pain." I answered not a word. He then took me by the hand to lead me, as I thought, to hell, when I cried out, "I will obey thee, Lord!" He then pointed my hand in different directions, and asked if I would go there. I replied, "Yes, Lord." He then led me, all the others following, till we came to a place where there was a great quantity of water, which looked like silver, where we made a

Section 70

halt. My hand was given to Christ, who led me into the water and stripped me of my clothing, which at once vanished from sight. Christ then appeared to wash me, the water feeling quite warm.

During this operation, all the others stood on the bank, looking on in profound silence. When the washing was ended, the sweetest music I had ever heard greeted my ears. We walked to the shore, where an angel stood with a clean, white robe, which the father at once put on me. In an instant I appeared to be changed into an angel. The whole company looked at me with delight, and began to make a noise which I called shouting. We all marched back with music. When we reached the tree to which the angel first led me, it hung full of fruit, which I had not seen before. The Holy Ghost plucked some and gave me, and the rest helped themselves. We sat down and ate of the fruit, which had a taste like nothing I had ever tasted before. When we had finished, we all arose and gave another shout. Then God and Father said to me: "You are now prepared, and must go where I have commanded you." I replied, "If I go, they will not believe me." Christ then appeared to write something with a golden pen and golden ink, upon golden paper. Then he

Section 71

rolled it up, and said to me: "Put this in your bosom, and, wherever you go, show it, and they will know that I have sent you to proclaim salvation to all." He then put it into my bosom, and they all went with me to a bright, shining gate, singing and shouting. Here they embraced me, and I found myself once more on earth.

When I came to myself, I found that several friends had been with me all night, and my husband had called a physician, but he had not been able to do anything for me. He ordered those around me to keep very quiet, or to go home. He returned in the morning, when I told him, in part, my story. He seemed amazed, but made no answer, and left me.

Several friends were in, during the day. While talking to them, I would, without thinking, put my hand into my bosom, to show them my letter of authority. But I soon found, as my friends told me, it was in my heart, and was to be shown in my life, instead of in my hand. Among other, my minister, Jehial C. Beman, came to see me. He looked very coldly upon me and said: "I guess you will find out your mistake before you are many months older." He was a scholar, and a fine speaker; and the sneering, indifferent way in which he addressed me, said most plainly:

Section 72

"You don't know anything." I replied: "My gifts are very small, I know, but I can no longer be shaken by what you or anyone else may think or say."

CHAPTER XIX

Public Effort—Excommunication

From this time the opposition to my life work commenced, instigated by the minister, Mr. Beman. Many in the church were anxious to have me preach in the hall, where our meetings were held at that time, and were not a little astonished at the minister's cool treatment of me. Strength two of the trustees got some of the elder sisters to call on the minister and ask him to let me preach. His answer was: "No; she can't preach her holiness stuff here, and I am astonished that you should ask it of me." The sisters said he seemed to be in quite a rage, although he said he was, not angry.

There being no meeting of the society on Monday evening, a brother in the church

Section 73

opened his house to me, that I might preach, which displeased Mr. Beman very much. He appointed a committee to wait upon the brother and sister who had opened their doors to me, to tell them they must not allow any more meetings of that kind, and that they must abide by the rules of the church, making them believe they would be excommunicated if they disobeyed him. I happened to be present at this interview, and the committee remonstrated with me for the course I had taken. I told them my business was with the Lord, and wherever I found a door opened intended to go in and work for my Master.

There was another meeting appointed at the same place, which I, of course, attended; after which the meetings were stopped for that time, though I held many more there after these people had withdrawn from Mr. Beman's church.

I then held meetings in my own house; whereas the minister told the members that if they attended them he would deal with them, for they were breaking the rules of the church. When he found that I continued the meetings, and that the Lord was blessing my feeble efforts, he sent a committee of two to ask me if I considered myself a member of his church. I told them I did, and should

Section 74

continue to do so until I had done something worthy of dismembership.

At this, Mr. Began sent another committee with a note, asking me to meet him with the committee, which I did. He asked me a number of questions, nearly all of which I have forgotten. One, however, I do remember: he. asked if I was willing to comply with the rules of the discipline. To this I answered: "Not if the discipline prohibits me from doing what God has bidden me to do; I fear God more than man." Similar questions were asked and answered in the same manner. The committee said what they wished to say, and then told me I could go home. When I reached the door, I turned and said: "I now shake of the dust of my feet as a witness against you. See to it that this meeting does not rise in judgment against you." The next evening, one of the committee came to me and told me that I was no longer a member of the church, because I had violated the rules of the discipline by preaching.

When this action became known, the people wondered how anyone could be excommunicated for trying to do good. I did not say much, and my friends simply said I had done nothing but hold meetings. Others, anxious to know the particulars, asked the minister

Section 75

what the trouble divas. He told them he had given me the privilege of speaking or preaching as long as I chose, but that he could not give me the right to use the pulpit, and that I was not satisfied with any other place. Also, that I had appointed meeting on the evening of his meetings, which was a thing no member had a right to do. For these reasons he said he had turned me out of the church.

Now, if the people who repeated this to me told the trust—and I have no doubt but they did—Mr. Beman told an actual falsehood. I had never asked for his pulpit, but had told him and others, repeatedly, that I did not care where I stood—any corner of the hall would do. To which Mr. Beman had answered: "You cannot have any place in the hall." Then I said: "I'll preach in a private house." He answered me: "No, not in this place; I am stationed over all Boston." He was determined I should not preach in the city of Boston. To cover up his deceptive, unrighteous course toward me, he told the above falsehoods.

From his statements, many erroneous stories concerning me gained credence with a large number of people. At that time, I thought it my duty as well as privilege to address a letter to the Conference, which I took to them in

Section 76

person, stating all the facts. At the same time I told them it was not in the power of Mr. Beman, or anyone else, to truthfully bring anything against my moral or religious character—that my only offence was in trying to preach the Gospel of Christ—and that I cherished no ill feelings toward Mr. Beman or anyone else, but that I desired the Conference to give the case an impartial hearing, and then give me a written statement expressive of their opinion., I also said I considered myself a member of the Conference, and should do so until they said I was not, and gave me their reasons, that I slight let the, world know what my offence had been.

My letter was slightingly noticed, and then thrown under the table. Why should they notice it? It was only the grievance of a woman, and there was no justice meted out to women in those days. Even ministers of Christ did not feel that women had any rights which they were bound to respect.

CHAPTER XX

Women in the Gospel

Thirty years ago there could scarcely a person be found, in the churches, to sympathize with anyone who talked of Holiness. But, in my simplicity, I did think that a body of Christian ministers would understand my case and judge righteously. I was, however, disappointed.

It is no little thing to feel that every man's hand is against us, and ours against every man, as seemed to be the case with me at this: time; yet how precious, if Jesus but be with us. In this severe trial I had constant access:. to God, and a clear consciousness that he heard me; yet I did not seem to have that plenitude of the Spirit that I had before. I realized most keenly that the closer the communion that may have existed, the keener the suffering of the slightest departure from God. Unbroken communion can only be retained by a constant application of the blood which cleanseth.

Section 78

Though I did not wish to pain any one, neither could I please any one only as I was let by the Holy Spirit. I saw, as never before, that the best men were liable to err, and that the only safe way was to fall on Christ, even though censure and reproach fell upon me for obeying his voice. Man's opinion weighed nothing with me, for my commission was from heaven, and my reward was with the Most High.

I could not believe that it was a short-lived impulse or spasmodic influence that impelled me to preach. I read that on the day of Pentecost was the Scripture fulfilled as found in Joel ii. 28, 29; and it certainly will not be denied that women as well as men were at that time pulled with the Holy Ghost, because it is expressly stated that women were among those who continued in prayer and supplication, waiting for the fulfillment of the promise. Women and men are classed together, and if the power to preach the Gospel is short-lived and spasmodic in the case of women, it must be equally so in that of men; and if women have lost the gift of prophecy, so have men.

We are sometimes told that if a woman pretends to a Divine call, and thereon grounds the right to plead the cause of a crucified Redeemer in public, she will be believed when she shows

Section 79

credentials from heaven; that is, when she works a miracle. If it be necessary to prove one's right to preach the Gospel, I ask of my brethren to show me their credentials, or I cannot believe in the propriety of their ministry.

But the Bible puts an end to this strife when it says: "There is neither male nor female in Christ Jesus." Philip had four daughters that prophesied, or preached. Paul called Priscilla, as well as Aquila, his "helper," or, as in the Greek, his "fellow-laborer." Rom. XV.3; 2 Cor. viii. 23; Phil. ii.5; 1 Thess. iii. 2. The same word, which, in our common translation, is now rendered a "servant of the church," in speaking of phebe (Rom. xix. 1), is rendered "minister" when applied to Tychicuss. Eph vi.21. When Paul said, "Help those women who labor with me in the Gospel," he certainly meant that they did more than to pour out tea. In the eleventh chapter of First Corinthians Paul gives directions, to men and women, how they should appear when they prophesy or pray in pubic assemblies; and he defines prophesying to be speaking to edification, exhoration and comfort.

I may further remark that the conduct of holy women ids recorded in scripture as an example to others of their sex. And in the early ages of christianity many women were

Section 80

happy and glorious in martyrdom. How nobly, how heroically, too, in later ages, have women suffered persecution and death for the name of, the Lord Jesus.

In looking over these facts, I could see no miracle wrought for those women more than in myself.

Though opposed, I went forth laboring for God, and he owned and blessed my labors, and has done so wherever I have been until this day. And while I walk obediently, I know he will, though hell may rage and vent its spite.

CHAPTER XXI

The Lord Leadeth—Labor in Philadelphia

As I left the Conference, God wonderfully filled my heart with his love, so that, as I passed from place to place, meeting one and another of the ministers, my heart went out in love to each of them as though he had been my father; and the language of 1 Pet i. 7, came forcibly to my mind: "The trial of our faith is much more precious than of gold that perisheth, though it be tried by fire." Fiery trials are not strange things to the Lord's anointed. The rejoicing in them is born only of the Holy Spirit. Oh, praise his holy name for a circumcised heart, teaching us that each trial of our faith hath its commission from the Father of spirits. Each wave of trial bears the Galilean Pilot on its crest. Listen: his voice is in the storm, and' winds and waves obey that voice: "It is I; be not afraid." He has promised us help and safety in the fires, and not escape from them.

Section 82

"And hereby we know that he abideth in us, by the Spirit which he hath gives us." 1 John iii. 24. Glory to the Lamb for the witness of the Holy Spirit! He knoweth that every step I have taken has been for the glory of God and the good of souls. However much I may have erred in judgment, it has been the fault of my head and not of my heart. I sleep, but my heart waketh; bless the Lord.

Had this opposition come from the world, it would have seemed as nothing. But coming, as it did, from those who had been much blessed—blessed with me—and who had once been friends of mine, it touched a tender spot; and had it not been for the precious blood of Jesus, I should have been lost.

While in Philadelphia, attending the Conference, I became acquainted with three sisters who believed they were called to public labors in their Master's vineyard. But they had been so opposed, they were very much distressed and shrank from their duty. One of them professed sanctification. They had met with more opposition from ministers than from any one else.

After the Conference had adjourned, I proposed to these sisters to procure a place and hold a series of meetings. They were pleased with the idea, and were willing to help if I would take charge of the meetings. They apprehended some difficulty, as there had never been a meeting there under the sole charge of women. The language of my heart was:

"Only Thou my Leader be
And I still will follow Thee."

Trusting in my Leader, I went on with the work. I hired a large place in Canal street, and there we opened our meetings, which continued eleven nights, and over one Sabbath. The room was crowded every night—some coming to receive good, others to criticise, sneer, and say hard things against us.

One of the sisters left us after a day or two, fearing that the Church to which she belonged would disown her if she continued to assist us. We regretted this very much, but could only say, "An enemy hath done this."

These meetings were a time of refreshing from the presence of the Lord. Many were converted, and a few stepped into the fountain of cleansing.

Some of the ministers, who remained in the city after the Conference, attended our meetings, and occasionally asked us if we were organizing a new Conference, with a view of drawing out from the churches. This was simply to ridicule our meeting.

Section 84

We closed with a love-feast, which caused such a stir among the ministers and many of the church-members, that we could not imagine what the end would be. They seemed to think we had well nigh committed the unpardonable sin.

CHAPTER XXII

A Visit to my parents—Further Labors

Some of the dear sisters accompanied me to Flatbush, where I assisted in a bush meeting. The Lord met the people in great power, and I doubt not there are many souls in glory to-day praising God for that meeting.

From that place I went home to my father's house in Binghamton, N.Y. They were filled with joy to have me with them once more, after an absence of six years. As my mother embraced me, she exclaimed: "So you are a preacher, are you?" I replied: "So they say." "Well, Julia," said she, "when I first heard that you were a preacher, I said that I would rather hear you were dead." These words,

Section 85

coming so unexpectedly from my mother, filled me with anguish. Was I to meet opposition here, too? But my mother, with streaming eyes, continued: "My dear daughter, it is all past now. I have heard from those who have attend your meetings what the Lord has done for you, and I am satisfied."

My stay in Binghamton was protracted several months. I held meetings in and around the town, to the acceptance of the people, and, I trust, to the glory of God. I felt perfectly satisfied, when the time came for me to leave, that my work was all for the Lord, and my soul was filled with joy and thankfulness for salvation. Before leaving, my parents decided to move to Boston, which they did soon after.

I left Binghamton the first of February, 1855, in company with the Rev. Henry Johnson and his wife, for Ithaca, N. Y., where I labored a short time. I met with some opposition from one of the A. M. E. Church trustees, He said a woman should not preach in the church. Beloved, the God we serve fights all our battles, and before I left the place that trustee was one of the most faithful at my meetings, and was very kind to assist me on my journey when I left Ithaca. I stopped one night at Owego, at Brother Loyd's and I also stopped for a short time at Onondaga, returned

Section 86

to Ithaca on the 14th of February, and staid until the 7th of March, during which time the work of grace was greatly revived. Some believed and entered into the rest of full salvation, many were converted, and a number of backsliders were reclaimed. I held prayer meetings from house to house. The sisters formed a woman's prayer-meeting, and the whole church seemed to be working in unison for Christ.

March 7th I took the stage for Geneva, and, arriving late at night, went to a hotel. In the morning Brother Rosel Jeffrey took me to his house and left me with his wife. He was a zealous Christian, but she scoffed at religion, and laughed and made sport during family worship. I do not know, but hope that long ere this she has ceased to ridicule the cause or the followers of Christ. In the latter part of the day Brother Condell came and invited me to his house. I found his wife a pleasant Christian woman. Sabbath afternoon I held a meeting in Brother Condell's house. The colored people had a church which the whites had given them. It was a union church, to be occupied on alternate Sundays by the Methodists and Baptists.

According to arrangement, this Sunday evening was the time for the Methodists to

Section 87

occupy the church. The Rev. Dawsey, of Canandaigua, came to fill his appointment, but, when we arrived at the church, the Baptist minister, William Monroe, objected to our holding a meeting in the house that evening, and his members joined with him in his unchristian course. Rather than have any trouble, we returned to Brother Condell's house. The minister preached and I followed with a short exhortation. The Lord was present to bless. They made an appointment for me to preach at the union meeting-house on the following Tuesday evening.

Monday evening I went with some of the sisters to the church, where there was a meeting for the purpose of forming a moral reform society. After the meeting, Brother Condell asked the trustees if they had any objection to having me speak in the church the next evening. To this, Minister Monroe and another man—I had almost said a fiend in human shape—answered that they did not believe in women's preaching, and would not admit one in the church, striving hard to justify themselves from the Bible, which one of them held in his unholy hands.

I arose to speak, when Mr. Monroe interrupted me. After a few words I left the house.

Section 88

The next afternoon, while taking tea at the house of one of the sisters, Minister Monroe came in to tell me he heard that our brethren had said they would have the church for me if they had to "shed blood." He asked me if I wanted to have anything to do with a fight of that kind. I replied: "The weapons with which I fight are not carnal, and, if I go to a place and am invited to use the weapons God has given me, I must use them to his glory."

"Well," said he, "I shall be in the pulpit at an early hour, and will not leave it though they break my head."

"Mr. Monroe," said I, "God can take you from the pulpit without breaking your head." At this he became very much excited, and raved as if he were a madman. For two hours he walked the floor, talking and reading all the time. I made him no reply and tried not to notice him, and finally he left me.'

At the proper time we went to the church. It was full, but everything was in confusion. Mr. Monroe was in the pulpit. I saw at once that God could not be glorified in the midst of such a pandemonium; so I withdrew at once. I was told they kept up the contention until after ten o'clock. Mr. Monroe tried hard to get our trustees to sat I should not preach in

Section 89

the place, but they would give him no such promise.

As I was obliged to leave in a few days, to meet other appointments, our men procured a large house, where I held a meeting the next evening. All that attended were quiet and orderly; one man arose for prayers.

Dear sisters, who are in the evangelistic work now, you may think you have hard times; but let me tell you, I feel that the lion and lamb are lying down together, as compared with the state of things twenty-five or thirty years ago. Yes, yes; our God is marching on. Glory to his name!

CHAPTER XXIII

Indignities on Account of Color—
General Conference

I Reached Rochester on the 16th of March, where I remained three weeks, laboring constantly for my Master, who rewarded me in the salvation of souls. Here God visited me after the same manner he did Elijah, when Elijah prayed to die. He strengthened me and bid me go forward with the promises recorded in the first chapter of Joshua.

April 21st I bade good-bye to Brother John H. Bishop's people, who had entertained me while in Rochester, and went to Binghamton to visit my parents again. I found them all well, and labored constantly for the Lord while I was there. I remained at home until the 8th of May, when I once more started out on my travels for the Lord. There was but one passenger in the stage besides myself. He gave his name as White, seemed very uneasy, and, at each stopping place, he would say: "I am afraid the public will take me for an abolitionist

to-day;" thus showing his dark, slaveholding principles.

I staid one night in Oxford, at Mr. Jackson's. At six o'clock the next morning I took passage on the canal packet "Governor Seward," with Captain George Keeler. That night, at a late hour, I made my way into the ladie's cabin, and, finding an empty berth, retired. In a short time a man came into the cabin, saying that the berths in the gentlemen's cabin were all occupied, and he was going to sleep in the ladies' cabin. Then he pointed to me and said: "That nigger has no business here. My family are coming on board the boat at Utica, and they shall not come where a nigger is." They called the captain, and he ordered me to get up; but I did not stir, thinking it best not to leave the bed except by force. Finally they left me, and the man found lodging among the seamen, swearing vengeance on the "niggers."

The next night the boat stopped at a village, and the captain procured lodging for me at an inn. Thus I escaped further abuse from that, ungodly man.

The second night we reached Utica, where I staid over Sunday. Then I went to Schenectady, where I remained a few days, working for my Master. Then I went to Albany, my old

Section 92

home. Sunday afternoon I preached in Troy, and that Sunday evening in Albany, to a crowded house. There were many of my old friends and acquaintances in the audience. This was the most solemn and interesting meeting I ever held. The entire audience seemed moved to prayer and tears by the power of the Holy Ghost.

On May 21st I went to New York. During the year that followed I visited too large a number of places to mention in this little work.

I went from Philadelphia in company with thirty ministers and Bishop Brown, to attend the General Conference, which way held in Pittsburgh, Pa. The ministers chartered the conveyance, and we had a very pleasant and interesting journey. The discussions during the day and meetings at night, on the canal boat, were instructive and entertaining. A very dear sister, Ann M. Johnson, accompanied me. The grand, romantic scenery, which I beheld while crossing the Alleghany mountains, filled me with adoration and praise to the great Creator of all things. We reached Pittsburgh on the 4th of June, and the General Conference of the A. M. E. Church convened on the 6th of June. The Conference

Section 93

lasted two weeks, and was held with open doors.

The business common to such meetings was transacted with spirit and harmony, with few exceptions. One was, a motion to prevent Free Masons from ministering in the churches. Another, to allow all the women preachers to become members of the conferences. This caused quite a sensation, bringing many members to their feet at once. They all talked and screamed to the bishop, who could scarcely keep order. The Conference was so incensed at the brother who offered the petition that they threatened to take action against him.

I remained several weeks, laboring among the people, much to the comfort of my own soul, and, I humbly trust, to the upbuilding at my dear Master's kingdom. I found the people very kind and benevolent.

CHAPTER XXIV

Continued Labors—
Death of my Husband and Father

From Pittsburgh I went to Cincinnati, where I found a large number of colored people of different denominations. The Methodists had a very good meeting-house on Sixth street, below Broad street. The members appeared to enjoy religion, but were very much like the world in their external appearance and cold indifference toward each other.

The station and circuit joined in holding a camp-meeting. The minister urged me very strongly to attend, which I did. Several souls professed faith in Christ at this meeting, but only one was willing to receive him in all his fullness.

After this meeting I labored in quite a number of places in Ohio. At some places I was kindly received, at others I was not allowed to labor publicly.

While thus laboring far from home, the sad intelligence of my husband's death came to me so suddenly as to almost cause me to sink beneath the blow. But the arm of my dear, loving, heavenly Father sustained me, and I was enabled to say: "Though he slay me, yet will I trust in him." I immediately hastened home to Boston, where I learned the particulars of my husband's death, which occurred on ship-board several months before. None but the dear Lord knew what my feelings were. I dared not complain, and thus cast contempt on my blessed Saviour, for I knew he would not lay more upon me than I could bear. He knows how to deliver the godly out of temptation and affliction; all events belong to him. All we have to be careful for is, to know of a truth that Christ is formed in our hearts the hope of glory, and hath set up his kingdom there, to reign over every affection and desire. Glory to the Lamb, who giveth me power thus to live!

After arranging my affairs at home, I went to Albany, where my sister lived, staid a short time with her, and held some meetings there. Then I went to Bethlehem, where I held several meetings, one in the M. E. Church, which was arranged only after there had been considerable controversy about letting a woman preach in their house. From there I went to Troy, where I also held meetings. In each of

these places this "brand plucked from the burning" was used of God to his glory in saving precious souls. To his name be all the glory!

I spent one Sunday in Poughkeepsie, working for Jesus. I then went to New York, where I took the boat for Boston. We were detained some hours by one of the shafts breaking. I took a very severe cold by being compelled to sit on deck all night, in the cold, damp air—prejudice not permitting one of my color to enter the cabin except in the capacity of a servant. O Prejudice! thou cruel monster! wilt thou ever cease to exist? Not until all shall know the Lord, and holiness shall be written upon the bells of the horses—upon all things in earth as well as in heaven. Glory to the Lamb, whose right it is to reign!

Upon my arrival home I found my father quite ill. He was sick for several months, and I remained at home until after his death, which event took place in May, 1849. He bore his long, painful illness with Christian patience and resignation. Just before leaving us for the better world, he called each of his children that were present to his bedside, exhorting them to live here in such a manner that they might meet him in heaven. To me he said: "My dear daughter, be faithful to your heavenly

Section 97

calling, and fear not to preach full salvation." After some precious words to his weeping wife, my dear father was taken to his eternal rest. Bless the Lord, O my soul, for an earnest, christian father! Reader, I trust it is your lot to have faithful, believing parents.

CHAPTER XXV

Work in Various Places

June 18th, 1849, I bade my mother and family farewell, and started out on my mission again. I stopped in New York, where I was joined by Sister Ann M. Johnson, who became my traveling companion. We went to Philadelphia, where we were entertained by Brother and Sister Lee. The dear, kind friends welcomed us warmly. Sister Johnson did not feel moved to labor in public, except to sing, pray, and recount her experience. I labored constantly while in this city, going from church to church.

On the 28th we went to Snow Hill, where we spent one Sunday. We visited Fethersville,

Section 98

Bordentown, Westchester and Westtown, all to the glory of God. I must say, the dear Holy Spirit wonderfully visited the people in all these places. Many were converted, and, now and then, one would step into the fountain of cleansing.

July 20th we left for New York, stopping at Burlington, Trenton, Princeton, Rahway, Brunswick and Newark. In each of these places we spent several days, much to our comfort and the apparent good of the churches. We arrived in New York city August 3d, and went to Bridgeport (Conn.) by boat. We found the church there in a very unsettled condition because of unbelief. We next went to New Haven, where we had some precious meetings. In Providence, R. I., we also received God's blessing on our labors.

At this time I received a pressing invitation from Rev. Daniel A. Paine, who is now bishop of the A. M. E. Church, to visit Baltimore, which I accepted. Upon our arrival there we were closely questioned as to our freedom, and carefully examined for marks on our persons by which to identify us if we should prove to be runaways. While there, a daughter of the lady with whom we boarded ran away from her self-styled master. He came, with others, to her mother's house at midnight, burst in

Section 99

the door without ceremony, and swore the girl was hid in the house, and that he would have her, dead or alive. They repeated this for several nights. They often came to our bed and held their light in our faces, to see if the one of whom they were looking was not with us. The mother was, of course, in great distress. I believe they never recovered the girl. Thank the dear Lord we do not have to suffer such indignities now, though the monster, Slavery, is not yet dead in all its forms.

We remained sometime in Baltimore, laboring mostly in Brother Paine's charge. We then went to Washington, D.C., where our conference was in session. The meetings were excellent, and great good was being done, when an incident occurred which cast a gloom over the whole Conference. One day, when a number of the ministers, Sister Johnson and myself, were dining at the house of one of the brethren, a slaveholder came and searched the house for a runaway. We realized more and more what a terrible thing it was for one human being to have absolute control over another.

We remained in Washington a few weeks, laboring for Christ. Although, at the time, it seemed as though Satan ruled there supreme, God gave us to know that his righteousness

Section 100

was being set up in many hearts. Glory to his excellent name.

The larger portion of the past year had been a time of close trial, yet I do not recollect ever closing a year more fully in Christ than I did that one. On taking a retrospective view of it, I found great cause for humiliation as well as thankfulness. I was satisfied with the Lord's dealings with me; my mind was kept in peace, while many had declined on the right hand and on the left; I was thankful that any were spared to bear the standard of the Redeemer.

Since I first entered the vineyard of my divine Master, I have seen many a star fall, and many a shining light go out and sink into darkness. Many, who have been singularly owned and blessed of God, have deserted his standard in the day of trial; yet, through his abounding grace, have I been kept. Glory be to the keeping power of the blood that cleanseth me, even me, from all sin!

CHAPTER XXVI

Further Labors—A "Threshing" Sermon

In June, 1850, I crossed the Alleghany mountains the second time. I was very sick on the journey and on arriving in Pittsburgh, was not able to sit up. Finding me in a raging fever, my friends called in a physician, and, as I continued to grow worse, another one. For three weeks my life was despaired of; and finally, on beginning to recover, it was many months before I felt quite well. In this severe affliction grace wonderfully sustained me. Bless the Lord!

I was advised to go down the Ohio river for the benefit of my health. Therefore, as soon as I was able to do so, I started for Cincinnati. I staid there several weeks with some friends by the name of Jones. The Lord so Strengthened me, that in a few months, I was able to resume my labors.

In October we went to Columbus. We labored there and in that vicinity for some time, content that in our protracted effort quite a number were converted. There were three persons there who said they had once enjoyed the blessing of sanctification, but were not then clear in the experience. Oh, how few are advocates for full salvation! Some will hold the whole truth in profession when and where it is not opposed, but, if they must become fools for the truth's sake, they compromise with error. Such have not and will not come to the perfect rest and inheritance of the saints on earth.

In April, 1851, we visited Chillicothe, and had some glorious meetings there. Great crowds attended every night, and the altar was crowded with anxious inquirers. Some of the deacons of the white people's Baptist church invited me to preach in their church, but I declined to do so, on account of the opposition of the pastor, who was very much set against women's preaching. He said so much against it, and against the members who wished me to preach, that they called a church meeting, and I heard that they finally dismissed him.

The white Methodists invited me to speak for them, but did not want the colored people to attend the meeting. I would not agree to any such arrangement, and, therefore, I did

not speak for them. Prejudice had closed the door of their sanctuary against the colored people of the place, virtually saying: "The Gospel shall not be free to all." Our benign Master and Saviour said: "Go, preach my Gospel to all."

We visited Zanesville, Ohio, laboring for white and colored people. The white methodists opened their house for the admission of colored people for the first time. Hundreds were turned away at each meeting, unable to get in; and, although the house was so crowded, perfect order prevailed. We also held meetings on the other side of the river. God the Holy Ghost was powerfully manifest in all these meetings. I was the recipient of many mercies, and passed through various exercises. In all of them I could trace the hand of God and claim divine assistance whenever I most needed it. Whatever I needed, by faith I had. Glory! glory!! While God lives, and Jesus sits on his right hand, nothing shall be impossible unto me, if I hold fast faith with a pure conscience.

On the 27th we went to Detroit, Mich. On the way, Sister Johnson had a very severe attack of ague, which lasted for several weeks. My soul had great liberty for God while laboring in this place.

Section 104

One day, quite an influential man in the community, though a sinner, called on me and appeared deeply concerned about his soul's welfare. He urged me to speak from Micah iv. 13: "Arise and thresh, O daughter of Zion," etc. I took his desire to the Lord, and was permitted to speak from that passage after this manner: 710 B.C. corn was threshed among the Orientals by means of oxen or horses, which were driven round an area filled with loose sheaves. By their continued tramping the corn was separated from the straw. That this might be done the more effectually, the text promised an addition to the natural horny substance on the feet of these animals, by making the horn iron and the hoof brass.

Corn is not threshed in this manner by us, but by means of flails, so that I feel I am doing no injury to the sentiment of the text by changing a few of the terms into those which are the most familiar to us now. The passage portrays the Gospel times, though in a more restricted sense it applies to the preachers of the word. Yet it has a direct reference to all God's people, who were and are commanded to arise and thresh. Glory to Jesus! now is this prophecy fulfilled—Joel ii. 28 and 29. They are also commanded to go to God, who alone is able to qualify them for their

Section 105

labors by making their horns iron and their hoofs brass. The Lord was desirous of imparting stability and perpetuity to his own divine work, by granting supernatural aid to the faithful that they might perform for him those services for which their own feeble and unassisted powers were totally inadequate. More than this, it is encouraging to the saints to know that they are provided with weapons both offensive and defensive.

The threshing instrument is of the former description. It is of the same quality as that which is quick and powerful and sharper than any two-edged sword. "For this purpose the Son of God was manifested, that he might destroy the works of the devil," and this is one of the weapons which he employs in the hands of his people to carry his gracious designs into execution, together with the promise that they shall beat in pieces many people. Isa. xxiii. 18; lx. 6-9.

There are many instances of the successful application of the Gospel flail, by which means the devil is threshed out of sinners. With the help of God, I am resolved, O sinner, to try what effect the smart strokes of this threshing instrument will produce on thy unhumbled soul. This is called the sword of the Spirit, and is in reality the word of God.

Such a weapon may seem contemptible in the eyes of the natural man; yet, when it is powerfully wielded, the consequences are invariably potent and salutary. Bless God! the Regulator says: "They overcame by the blood of the Lamb and by the word of their testimony; and they loved not their lives unto the death." The atonement is the greatest weapon. In making trial of its efficacy, little children have caused the parent to cry aloud for mercy; but, in every case, much of its heavenly charm and virtue depends upon the mode in which it is applied.

This Gospel flail should be lifted up in a kind and loving spirit. Many shrink at sight of the flail, and some of us know, by blessed experience, that when its smart strokes are applied in the power and demonstration of the Holy Spirit, it causes the very heart to feel sore and painful. Penitent soul, receive the castigation, and you will feel, after it, like saying: "Now let me be crucified, and this work of the devil, inbred sin, put to death, that Christ may live and reign in me without a rival."

To the glory of God I wish to say, that the unconverted man, who gave me the text for the above discourse, gave his heart to God, together with many others, before we left

Detroit. In after years I was informed of his happy death. Praise the Lord for full and free salvation! Reader, have you this salvation—an ever-flowing fountain—in your soul? God grant it. Amen!

CHAPTER XXVII

My Cleveland Home—Later Labors

In June 1851, we went to Canada, where we were kindly received. We labored in different churches with great success. We found many living Christians there—some holding high the light of full salvation, and others willing to be cleansed. After spending a few weeks there, we crossed to Buffalo, but did not make any stay there at that time.

The places visited during that year are too numerous to mention here. Suffice it to say, the great Head of the Church went before us, clearing the way and giving us unmistakable evidence of his presence in every battle. Hallelujah!

Section 108

We returned to Columbus to fill an appointment which was awaiting us. After this, we made arrangements to go to Cleveland. One of the brethren engaged our passage and paid the fare, but we were not permitted to leave until four days afterward. At that time a colored person was not allowed to ride in the stage if any white passenger objected to it. There were objections made for three mornings, but, on the fourth, the stage called for us, and we had a safe journey to Cleveland. We expected to make a visit only, as in other cities; but the All-Father intended otherwise, and, more than twenty years ago, Cleveland became my home. After settling down, we still continued to visit neighboring cities and labor for Christ.

It was about this time that I became afflicted with the throat difficulty, of which I shall speak later. Beloved, the dear Lord only knows how sorely I was tried and tempted over this affliction.

St. James speaks of temptations as being common to the most holy of men, and also as a matter of joy and rejoicing to such as are exercised thereby, if so be they are not overcome by them. I think all temptation has a tendency to sin, but all temptation is not sin. There is a diversity of temptations, and a

Section 109

diversity of causes from which temptations proceed. Some come immediately from our corrupt nature, and are in themselves sinful. Others arise from the infirmity of our nature, and these every Christian has to contend with so long as he sojourns in a tabernacle of clay. There are also temptations which come directly from the enemy of souls. These our blessed Lord severely labored under, and so do the majority of his children. "Blessed is the man that endureth temptation"!

During the years that I rested from my labors and tried to recover my health, God permitted me to pass through the furnace of trial, heated seven times hotter than usual. Had not the three-one God been with me, I surely must have gone beneath the waves. God permits afflictions and persecutions to come upon his chosen people to answer various ends.

Sometimes for the trial of their faith, and the exercise of their patience and resignation to his will, and sometimes to draw them off from all human dependence, and to teach them to trust in Him alone. Sometimes he suffers the wicked to go a great way, and the ungodly to triumph over us, that he may prove our steadfastness and make manifest his power in upholding us. Thus it was with me. I had trusted too much in human wisdom, and

Section 110

God suffered all these things to come upon me. He upheld me by his grace, freeing me from all care or concern about my health or what man could do. He taught me to sit patiently, and wait to hear my Shepherd's voice; for I was resolved to follow no stranger, however plausibly he might plead.

I shall praise God through all eternity for sending me to Cleveland, even though I have been called to suffer.

In 1856, Sister Johnson, who had been my companion during all these years of travel, left me for her heavenly home. She bore her short illness without a murmur, resting on Jesus. As she had lived, so she died, in the full assurance of faith, happy and collected to the last, maintaining her standing in the way of holiness without swerving either to the right or to the left. Glory to the blood that keeps us!.

My now sainted mother, who was then in feeble health, lived with me in Cleveland for a few years. As the time for her departure drew near, she very much desired to visit her two daughters—One in Albany, the other in Boston. I feared she was not able to endure the journey, but her desire was so strong, and her confidence in God so great that he would spare her to see her girls again, that I finally consented

that she should undertake the journey I put her in charge of friends who were going cost, and she reached my sister's house in safety. She had been with them but a few weeks, when she bade them a long farewell and passed peacefully to heaven. I shall see her again where parting is unknown.

The glorious wave of holiness, which has been rolling through Ohio during the past few years, has swept every hindrance out of my way, and sent me to sea once more with chart and compass.

> "The Bible is my chart; it is a chart and compass too,
> Whose needle points forever true."

When I drop anchor again, it will be in heaven's broad bay.

Glory to Jesus for putting into my hand that precious, living light, *"The Christian Harvester."* May it and its self-sacrificing editor live many years, reflecting holy light as they go.

If anyone arise from the perusal of this book, scoffing at the word of truth which he has read, I charge him to prepare to answer for the profanation at the peril of his soul.

CHAPTER XXVIII

A Word to my Christian Sisters

Dear Sisters : I would that I could tell you; a hundredth part of what God has revealed to me of his glory, especially on that never-to-be-forgotten night when I received my high and holy calling. The songs I heard I think were those which Job, David and Isaiah speak of hearing at night upon their beds, or the one of which the Revelator says "no man could learn." Certain it is, I have not been able to sing it since, though at times I have seemed to hear the distant echo of the music. When I tried to repeat it, it vanished in the direct distance. Glory! glory! glory to the Most High!

Sisters, shall not you and I unite with the heavenly host in the grand chorus? If so, you will not let what man may say or do, keep you from doing the will of the Lord or using the gifts you have for the good of others. How much easier to bear the reproach of men

than to live at a distance from God. Be not kept in bondage by those who say, "We suffer not a woman to teach," thus quoting Paul's words, but not rightly applying them. What though we are called to pass through deep waters, so our anchor is cast within the veil, both sure and steadfast? Blessed experience! I have had to weep because this was not my constant experience. At times, a cloud of heaviness has covered my mind, and disobedience has caused me to lose the clear witness of perfect love.

One time I allowed my mind to dwell too much on my physical condition. I was suffering severely from throat difficulty, and took the advice of friends, and sought a cure from earthly physicians, instead of applying to the Great Physician. For this reason my joy was checked, and I was obliged to cease my public labors for several years. During all this time I was less spiritual, less zealous, yet I was not willing to accept the suggestion of Satan, that I had forfeited the blessing of holiness. But alas! the witness was not clear, and God suffered me to pass through close trials, tossed by the billows of temptation.

Losing my loving husband just at this time, I had much of the world to struggle with and against.

Section 114

Those who are wholly sanctified need not fear that God will hide his face, if they continue to walk in the light even as Christ is in five light. Then they have fellowship with the Father and the Son, and become of one spirit with the Lord. I do not believe God ever withdraws himself from a soul which does not first withdraw itself from him, though such may abide union cloud for a season, and have to cry: "My God! my God! why hast thou forsaken me?"

Glory to God, who giveth us the victory through our Lord Jesus Christ! His blood meets all the demands of the law against us. It is the blood of Christ that sues for the fulfillment of his last will and testament, and brings down every blessing into the soul.

When I had well nigh despaired of a cure from my bodily infirmities, I cried from the depths of my soul for the blood of Jesus to be applied to my throat. My faith laid hold of the precious promises—John xiv 14; Mark ii. 23; xi.24. At once I ceased trying to join the iron and the clay—the truth of God with the sayings and advice of men. I looked to my God for a fresh act of his sanctifying power. Bless his name! deliverance did come, with the balm, and my throat has troubled me but little since. This was ten years ago. Praise

Section 115

the Lord for that holy fire which many waters of trial and temptation cannot quench.

Dear sisters in Christ, are any of you also without understanding and slow of heart to believe, as were the disciples? Although they had seen their Master do many mighty works, yet, with change of place or circumstances, they would go back upon the old ground of carnal reasoning and unbelieving fears. The darkness and ignorance of our natures are such, that, even after we have embraced the Saviour and received his teaching, we are ready to stumble at the plainest truths! Blind unbelief is always sure to err; it is neither trace God nor trust him. Unbelief is ever alive to distrust and fear. So long as this evil root has a place in us, our fears cannot be removed nor our hopes confirmed.

Not till the day of Pentecost did Christ's chosen ones see clearly, or have their understandings opened; and nothing short of a full baptism of the Spirit will dispel our unbelief. Without this, we are but babes—all our lives are often carried away by our carnal natures and kept in bondage; whereas, if we are wholly saved and live under the full sanctifying influence of the Holy Ghost, we cannot be tossed about with every wind, but, like an iron pillar or a house built upon a rock, prove

Section 116

immovable. Our minds will then be fully illuminated, our hearts purified, and our souls filled with the pure love of God, bringing forth fruit to his glory.

CHAPTER XXIX

Love not the World

"If and man love the world, the love of the Father is not in him." John ii. 15. The spirit which is in the world is widely different from the Spirit which is of God; yet many vainly imagine they can unite the two. But as we read in Luke x. 26, so it is between the spirit of the world and the Spirit which is of God. There is a great gulf fixed between them—a gulf which cuts off all union and intercourse; and this gulf will eternally prevent the least degree of fellowship in spirit.

If we be of God and have the love of the Father in our hearts, we are not of the world, because whatsoever is of the world is not of God. We must be one or the other. We cannot unite heaven and hell—light and darkness

Section 116

Worldly honor, wordly pleasure, worldly grandeur, worldly designs and worldly pursuits are all incompatible with the love of the Father and with that kingdom of righteousness, peace and joy in the Holy Ghost, which is not of the world, but of God. Therefore, God says: "Be not conformed to the world, but be ye transformed by the renewing of your mind, that ye may prove what is that good, and acceptable and perfect will of God." Rom.xii.2.

As we look at the professing Christians of to-day, the question arises, Are they not all conformed to the maxims and fashions of this world, even many of those who profess to have been sanctified? But they say the transforming and renewing here spoken of means, as it says, the mind, not the clothing. But, if the mind be renewed, it must affect the clothing. It is by the Word of God we are to be judged, not by our opinion of the Word; hence, to the law and the testimony. In a like manner the Word also says: "That women adorn themselves in modest apparel, with shamefacedness and sobriety, not with bordered hair, or gold, or pearls, or costly array, but which becometh a woman professing godliness, with good works." 1 Tim. ii.9, 10; 1 Pet. iii. 3-5. I might quote many passages to the same effect,

Section 118

if I had time or room. Will you not hunt them up, and read carefully and prayerfully for yourselves?

Dear Christians, is not the low state of pure religion among all the churches the result of this worldly-mindedness? There is much outward show; and doth not this outward show portend the sore judgments of God to be executed upon the ministers and members? Malachi ii.7, says: "The priest's lips should keep knowledge," etc. But it is a lamentable fact that too many priests' lips speak vanity. Many profess to teach, but few are able to feed the lambs, while the sheep are dying for lack of nourishment and the true knowledge of salvation.

The priests' office being to stand between God and the people, they ought to know the mind of God toward his people—what the acceptable and perfect will of God is. Under the law, it was required that the priests should be without blemish—having the whole of the inward and outward as complete, uniform and consistent as it was possible to be under that dispensation; thereby showing the great purity that is required by God in all those who approach near unto him. "Speak unto Aaron and his sons that they separate themselves," etc. The Lord here gives a charge to

Section 119

the priests, under a severe penalty, that in all their approaches they shall sanctify themselves. Thus God would teach his ministers. and people that he is a holy God, and will be worshipped in the beauty of holiness by all those who come into his presence.

Man may fill his office in the church outwardly, and God may in much mercy draw nigh to the people when devoutly assembled to worship him; but. if the Minister has not had previous recourse to the fountain which is opened for sin and uncleanness, and felt the sanctifying and renewing influences of the Holy Ghost, he will feel himself shut out from these divine communications. Oh, that God may baptize the ministry and church with the Holy Ghost and with fire.

By the baptism of fire the church must be purged from its dead forms and notions respecting the in being of sin in all believers till death. The Master said: "Now ye are clear through the word which I have spoken unto you; abide in me," etc. Oh! blessed union. Christian, God wants to establish your heart unblamable in holiness. 1 Thess. i. 13; iv.7; Heb. xii.

14; Rom. vi.19. Will you let him do it, by putting away all filthiness of the flesh as well as of the spirit? "Know ye not that ye are the temple of God?" etc. 1 Cor. iii. 16,

17; 2 Cor. vi. 16, 17. Thus we will continue to search and find what the will of God is concerning his children. 1 Thess. vi. 3,4. Bless God! we may all have that inward, instantaneous sanctification, whereby the root, the inbeing of sin, is destroyed.

Do not misunderstand me. I am not teaching absolute perfection, for that belongs to God alone. Nor do I mean a state of angelic or Adamic perfection, but Christian perfection—an extinction of every temper contrary to love.

"Now, the God of peace sanctify you wholly—your whole spirit, soul and body. 2 Thess. v. 23. Glory to the blood!" "Faithful is he that calleth you, who also will do it." Paul says: He is able to do exceeding abundantly, above all that we ask or think. Eph. iii. 20.

Beloved reader, remember that you cannot commit sin and be a Christian, for "He that committeth sin is of the devil!". If you are regenerated, sin does not reign in your mortal body but if you are sanctified, sin does not exist in you. The sole ground of our perfect peace from all the carnal mind is by the blood of Jesus, for he is our peace, whom God hath set forth to be a propiation, through faith in his blood. "By whom also we have access by faith into this grace where in we stand"—having entered into the holiest by the blood of Jesus.

Let the blood be the sentinel, keeping the tempter without, that you may have constant peace within; for Satan cannot swim in still, waters. Isa. xxx. 7.

CHAPTER XXX

How to obtain Sanctification

How is sanctification to be obtained? An important question. I answer, by faith. Faith is the only condition of sanctification. By this I mean a faith that dies out to the world and every form of sin; that gives up the sin of the heart; and that believes, according to God's promise, he is able to perform, and will do it now—doeth it now.

Why not yield, believe, and be sanctified now—now, while reading? "Now is the day of salvation." Say: "Here, Lord, I will, I do believe; thou hast said now—now let it be—now apply the blood of Jesus to my waiting, longing soul."

> "Hallelujah! 'tis done!
> I believe on the Son;
> I am saved by the blood
> Of the crucified One."

Holy is the Lamb

Mrs. J.A. foote . . . E.A. Hoffman

1. Mixture of joy and sor-row daily do I pass through;

2. Sometimes I am ex-alt-ed, On eagle's wings I fly;

3. Sometimes I am indoubting, And think I have no grace;

Sometimes I'am in the valley, Then sinking down with woe.

Ris-ing above Mount Pisgah, I almost reach the sky.

Sometimes I am a-shouting, And camp-meeting is the place.

CHORUS.

Holy, holy, holy is the Lamb, Who saves me from all sin, from all [my sin!

Holy, holy, holy is the lamb, Whose blood doth make me clean!

4. sometimes, when I am praying,

It almost sems a task;

Sometimes I get a blessing,

The greatest I can ask.

5. Sometimes I read by Bible,

It almost seems a task;

Sometimes I find a blessing

Wherever I do look.

6. O, why am I thus tossed

Thus tossed to and fro?

Because the blood of Jesus

Hasn't washed me white as snow.

7. Oh, come to Christ, the Savior,

Drink of that living stream;

Your thirst he'll quench forever

And cleanse you from all sin.

Section 124

Now, dear reader, I conclude by praying that this little work may be blessed of God to your spiritual and everlasting good. I trust also that it will promote the cause of holiness in the Church.

Now, unto Him who is able to do exceeding abundantly, above all that we ask or think, according to the power that worketh in us; unto Him be glory in the church by Christ Jesus throughout all ages, world without end. Amen.

COMMENTARY

This portion of the book analyzes and comments on the various autobiographical chapters as I note them as sections of the Foote book. The analysis is done to view the Foote book through contemporary, 21st century eyes. The narrative by Foote is well written and provides a 19th century view of her personal experiences as a woman called to ministry. The autobiographical narrative also provides a view of African American history, history of the A.M.E. Church, the Holiness Movement, and many notable people of color from the 1800's that were Julia Foote's contemporaries. The commentary provides items of reflection to women who are called to ministry, actively serving in ministry, and those that just aren't sure if they are called to preach the Gospel.

Dietrich Bonhoeffer in his book "The Cost of Discipleship" concludes that following Jesus is not an easy road. It is one of personal sacrifice and even misery at times. In other words there is a cost. Being obedient and faithful to God cost Jesus His life, but it was a life that was gladly laid down to fulfill God's salvific purpose and plan for humanity.

The quotes below by Bonhoeffer indicate that following Jesus is a matter of God's grace which is in every case sufficient. But, man seeks cheap grace to avoid discipleship that is fraught with discipline, trials and hardships which are necessary to follow Jesus Christ.

Bonhoeffer quote:

"Costly grace is the gospel which must be sought again and again and again, the gift which must be asked for, the door at which a man must knock. Such grace is costly because it calls us to follow, and it is grace because it calls us to follow Jesus Christ. It is costly because it costs a man his life, and it is grace because it gives a man the only true life. It is costly because it condemns sin, and grace because it justifies the sinner. Above all, it is costly because it cost God the life of his Son: 'Ye were bought at a price', and what has cost God much cannot be cheap for us. Above all, it is grace because God did not reckon his Son too dear a price to pay for our life, but delivered him up for us. Costly grace is the Incarnation of God."

Bonhoeffer quote:

"Cheap grace is the grace we bestow on ourselves. Cheap grace is the preaching of forgiveness without requiring repentance, baptism without church discipline, Communion without confession . . . . Cheap grace is grace without discipleship, grace without the cross, and grace without Jesus Christ, living and incarnate."

Commentary Analysis:

As you read the autobiographical sketch of Julia A. J. Foote an analysis of each section (chapter) is provided. The analysis defines some 19th century terms, and emphasizes some ministerial reflective thoughts by the commentators.

Section 10:

A **public house** is believed to have been a "pub" or drinking establishment that sometimes had rooms.

Section 11:

M.E. Church is the Methodist Episcopal Church.

"Mother in Israel" first appears in the song of Deborah that describes the travail of the people under Jabin, the king of Canaan, until Deborah, a mother in Israel, arose to lead them out of bondage (Judg. 5:2-31; cf. 2 Sam. 20:19). It is a title given to women that faithfully support the church and demonstrate formal or informal leadership in some capacity.

Section 13:

This section describes an incident in which Julia (Julia A. J. Foote) as a child, prior to the age of eight, learned a lesson about sneaking and drinking liquor which made her sick, as well as, drunk. It is the first instances in which she describes being "like a brand plucked from the fire". It is this expression of sin that brings to mind the narrow escape that is made when sin does not lead to physical or eternal death. Julia recognizes her life was sparred.

Section 14:

Julia was taught the Lord's Prayer at the age of eight by a white woman and it was at that time that she believed she was converted. It was this prayer that filled her heart and made her hunger and thirst to know more of God. She strongly desired to learn to read even though there were no schools to teach colored children. It was her father who barely able to read himself took on the obligation to teach Julia to read one alphabetic letter at a time.

The impressions made to children by adults can be profound if positive. Introduction to prayer and Bible reading at a young age can fill a child with the awe of God's Word.

Section 18:

Julia's heart of compassion begins to unfold at the tender age of ten. Living with a family known as the Primes, she notices Mrs. Prime's brother is dying with consumption (tuberculosis) and her heart goes out to him. She begins to worry and wonder whether he is saved. This is the start to her quest for others to know the saving knowledge of Jesus Christ.

Section 19:

Julia began intercessory prayer at the age of ten for Mrs. Prime's brother who was dying from tuberculosis. Julia was fervent and consistent with prayer until the man died. It is such acts that set apart those that are called to God's service. A caring and compassionate heart; a solicitation of another's faith and salvation status; and prayer that intercedes on another's behalf are all characteristics of ministry.

Section 20:

Advice to parents is given based on the teaching of the Bible and personal experience. Even in the 1800's there was a concern that children were not being properly guided into Christian fellowship by their parents. Sunday's in the 1800's as in today were taken by children and allowed by parents for roving the streets or other sinful activities that did not prioritize God and church attendance for worship.

Section 21 – 23:

Julia learns that even horrendous acts must be met with a call for Christian discipleship. She determines that capital punishment must be banished. Julia at a young age does not know the Gospel fully but can interpret that love is needed more than hate, revenge, and retaliation.

It is amazing the impressions that are made on the young that last a lifetime. But, bad can lead to good in Jesus name. The dispensation of the gospel pours out love instead of an eye-for-an-eye.

Section 24 – 27:

Julia learns a hard lesson about false accusations. She feels the sting of evil and the humiliation of deception. It was a time for her to forgive but that did not come easy. At age twelve she could not forget or forgive the injustices done to her.

Section 28 – 29:

During adolescence Julia begins to value the world's pleasures more than her relationship with God. She could feel the tug of her heart as she disobeyed God and parents to seek as she puts it, "bartering the things of the kingdom for the fooleries of the world."

Section 30 – 31:

Julia witnesses a "super-natural" event as she is pulled from a dance floor by an invisible force. She is learning that God will not permit those called by His name to engage in sinful behaviors. If they will not on their own move away from sin, they can otherwise be persuaded by unexplainable forces.

Section 32 – 35:

Once again God acted in a mighty way towards Julia as she attended a church service and was convicted of her sin. She was overcome by the Holy Spirit and fell unconscious. During this state she could feel the depravity of her sin. But, the power of God overcame her and assured her of His love. Julia was converted through the power of the Holy Spirit and through her willingness to accept by faith the miraculous work God had done on her behalf.

But, then the deceiver tried to convince Julia that she was not saved. Seeds of doubt were planted in her mind. God came to her rescue through her church minister who assured her that she was saved based on faith and not by any outward actions she did or did not perform.

Julia hungered for the Word of God and began reading the Bible every spare moment. This is the dedication of a calling that drives a person to want to know more and more about his or her master, Jesus Christ.

Section 36 – 37:

Julia was kept from reading the Bible because she was reading it at night against her mother's knowledge so the Bible was taken away from her. But, God made a provision for Julia. Her church minister gave her a Bible.

Julia delighted in the Bible more than anything else. The Holy Spirit had upon Julia's asking for a Bible was given one. Julia began to be able to read and better understand the Bible.

Julia was given a setback when she lost her eyesight in one eye due to an accident. This was another opportunity for Satan to discourage Julia. But, Julia persevered knowing that she could not be foiled (fail or be defeated) because of her faith in God.

Trials come to make us stronger and even more determined. They provide maturity in Jesus Christ.

Section 38:

This section contains a warning and recognition by Julia about preaching which describes God's Word as mere history. Julia compared this description of the Bible as mere history as a dreadful occurrence similar to the **woe to shepherds of Israel** found in Ezekiel 34, which reads in verse 7 (NIV):

[7] "'Therefore, you shepherds, hear the word of the LORD: [8] As surely as I live, declares the Sovereign LORD, because my flock lacks a shepherd and so has been plundered and has become food for all the wild animals, and because my shepherds did not search for my flock but cared for themselves rather than for my flock, [9] therefore, you shepherds, hear the word of the LORD: [10] This is what the Sovereign LORD says: I am against the shepherds and will hold them accountable for my flock. I will remove them from tending the flock so that the shepherds can no longer

feed themselves. I will rescue my flock from their mouths, and it will no longer be food for them.

Section 39:

The hope to attend school seemed to be the only way that Julia would learn to read progressively better so that she could more fully understand the Bible. A school for coloreds was formed but quickly closed due to harassment by those who believed coloreds should not be educated. Once again the Holy Spirit brought peace and understanding to Julia as it helped her to understand the Bible even without formal schooling and she was calmed in her anxiety about wanting education.

Section 40 – 41:

Julia learned that those closest to her could at times be stumbling blocks for her. Her desire to know God more and more fully was discussed with her church minister and family. She was thought to be unreasonable and even crazed because of her unending desire to learn about God. Julia desired a "Philip" (as in the Bible in Acts chapter 8 when the Eunuch described to Philip his great desire to understand the Word of God and Philip interpreted God's Word for the Eunuch) to help her understand the Bible.

After hearing about sanctification, Julia sought sanctification believing it was what was lacking to help her in her struggles. She was prayed for by an elderly couple, which was compelled to help. Julia continued to go to her secret closet (behind the chimney in the garret (thought to be an attic) of her house) and prayed for sanctification and it was granted. The glory of God rested upon her almost prostrating her to the floor.

Section 42 – 45

As Julia told others of her sanctification she expected them to be joyous for her, but they resented her and did not believe her. How could a child be sanctified? This was a lesson to Julia and to all those who declare their calling and anointing by God. You will be rejected even by those that are family, friends, and Christians.

Several Scriptures were assuring to Julia. They included:
John 17
Thessalonians 4:3
1 Corinthians 6:9-12
Hebrews 2:11

Section 46 – 48:

Even Julia's church minister became uncomfortable with her declarations of sanctification and her desire to lead others to Christ. He insisted that she could not read and dictate God's Word to people that were older than she. But, this only quickened her spirit more and more. She wanted sanctification for everyone. Julia realized the great and wonderful thing that God had done in her life. She was like a brand snatched from the fire.

As time went on Julia was courted by a young man who made her an offer of marriage. She struggled with the thought because it would make her unequally yoked as the young man was not sanctified. He had professed faith in Christ, but was not sanctified (made Holy in Jesus Christ).

Section 49 – 50:

The young man that pursued Julia left for Boston, Massachusetts without receiving sanctification. Julia continued to pray for him. Hebrews 4:15 brought her great comfort, as she denounced the attacks of Satan that tried to get her to doubt her sanctification.

Hebrews 4:15 (NIV) reads, "For we do not have a high priest who is unable to empathize with our weaknesses, but we have one who has been tempted in every way, just as we are—yet he did not sin."

Section 51 – 52:

After a year apart the young man returned. Julia knew in some ways he still had a carnal mind, but believed he would be sanctified. Julia was married and moved to Boston with her new husband. Julia committed herself to Christ as she traveled to Boston professing, "I will gladly forsake all to follow thee." The move to Boston was just a little sacrifice as she left her mother and father, church, friends, and family and went where she believed God was taking her with her new husband.

Section 53 – 55:

Julia and her husband lodged in a boarding house and soon joined a church. Her testimony intrigued many people and they too wanted to be sanctified. Some people did not believe it was possible to live a sinless life and rejected her testimony. It was a "**foolish doctrine**" to them.

The fellowship of the believers sustained Julia and she never hesitated to share her testimony with others that they might come to know Jesus.

Section 56 – 58:

Julia met with and shared her testimony and many came to know Jesus and some did not. But, that did not discourage her. She witnessed a close friend receive sanctification and the supernatural moving of the Holy Spirit as her friend was near death and testified of the glory of God. The dying friend spoke of see God's chariots and horses that had come to receive her unto Him.

Section 59 – 61

Julia and her husband began to slowly drift apart as he could not understand her incessant quest for godliness. He accepted an offer to go to sea for six months. His departure brought difficulty to Julia as she struggled between disapprobation (disapproval) of his actions and Christian forbearance. God led her to a scripture in Isaiah chapter fifty-four that reads in verse, 5,

"for thy Maker is thy husband . . ." This scripture brought Julia peace as she purposed to glorify God.

Section 62 – 64:

Julia visited the poor and forsaken while her husband was at sea. She provided them with reading and talking to them of Jesus. On one occasion she heard a voice call her name. It was her older brother with which the family had lost touch. He was sick and dying. She asked him to pray for his salvation. He later died. Julia knew she did the right thing and only God knew her brother's fate.

Julia's husband enlisted for another tour at sea and Julia continued to follow God's leading in her life.

Section 65 – 67
Julia's Call to Preach

Julia was drawn to souls that needed salvation. It was at this time that God sent an angel to her with a scroll that read, "Thee I have chosen to preach my Gospel without delay." Julia was resistant. She did not think she could do it because of the difficulties of women and she also had resisted women preachers although she acknowledged that it was unfounded.

Julia's husband returned from sea and she told him about her calling to preach. As she resisted the call to preach she became weak and sick. She and others believed she would either die or go crazy. An angel visited her again confirming her call to preach God's Word. Julia began to read Hebrews chapter six again and again. Hebrews 6 (NIV) 4—20 reads:

[4] It is impossible for those who have once been enlightened, who have tasted the heavenly gift, who have shared in the Holy Spirit, [5] who have tasted the goodness of the word of God and the powers of the coming age [6] and who have fallen away, to be brought back to repentance. To their loss they are crucifying the Son of God all over again and subjecting him to public disgrace. [7] Land that drinks in the rain often falling on it and that produces a crop useful to those for whom it is farmed receives the

blessing of God. [8] But land that produces thorns and thistles is worthless and is in danger of being cursed. In the end it will be burned.

[9] Even though we speak like this, dear friends, we are convinced of better things in your case—the things that have to do with salvation. [10] God is not unjust; he will not forget your work and the love you have shown him as you have helped his people and continue to help them. [11] We want each of you to show this same diligence to the very end, so that what you hope for may be fully realized. [12] We do not want you to become lazy, but to imitate those who through faith and patience inherit what has been promised.

The Certainty of God's Promise

[13] When God made his promise to Abraham, since there was no one greater for him to swear by, he swore by himself, [14] saying, "I will surely bless you and give you many descendants"[15] And so after waiting patiently, Abraham received what was promised.

[16] People swear by someone greater than themselves, and the oath confirms what is said and puts an end to all argument. [17] Because God wanted to make the unchanging nature of his purpose very clear to the heirs of what was promised, he confirmed it with an oath. [18] God did this so that, by two unchangeable things in which it is impossible for God to lie, we who have fled to take hold of the hope set before us may be greatly encouraged. [19] We have this hope as an anchor for the soul, firm and secure. It enters the inner sanctuary behind the curtain, [20] where our

forerunner, Jesus, has entered on our behalf. He has become a high priest forever, in the order of Melchizedek.

You must read this section of the Foote autobiography for yourself. If you are inclined to believe you are called to ministry.

Section 68 – 72

Julia received yet more heavenly disitations (visit from an angel and supernatural occurrences). Two months after the first visitation Julia had another. This visitation took her to the very presence of God, Jesus Christ and the Holy Spirit. Once again her calling to preach was confirmed and she agreed to do so.

Julia was still bothered by the rejection she knew she would receive from family and friends. God gave her confidence as He led her through what she believed to be Heaven and imparted His desire for her as He stated, "warn the people of their sins in my name."

You must read this section for yourself. Commentary cannot make any clearer what is already stated by Julia.

It is at this time that as Julia confirmed her willingness to preach the Gospel that opposition to her life work commenced. First her church minister, **Jehiel C. Behman**, became cold towards her and began to instigate trouble. He was confounded that God could call her to ministry and refused to let her preach at the church.

But God opened a door for her to preach at a congregant's home. Julia then began to hold meetings at her own home in which she preached.

When it was apparent the Julia feared God more than man she was dismembered from her church. The congregants could not understand how she could be dismembered (church membership taken away) for trying to do good.

Jehiel C. Behman is a known 1800's Methodist (African Methodist Episcopal) minister and worker within abolitionist circles. His oppositional stance on women speaking in public places is well documented and not logically understood based on his work against oppression of coloreds.

Section 73 – 76:
Julia's minister not being able to intimidate her decided to destroy her by telling falsehoods about her and he indicated that he was powerful in the city of Boston and would prevent her from preaching anywhere in Boston.

The falsehoods included that Julia was offered to preach in the church, but she would not be permitted to preach from the pulpit. This was false as this offer was never made to Julia and Julia did not care whether she preached in the pulpit or from the floor.

Other falsehoods were also told by her minister. Julia as excommunicated from the church and her written plea to the conference were ignored. Julia concluded that women did not have any rights not even the right (from church ministers) to preach God's Word.

Section 77 – 80

In this section Julia defends women in the Gospel. She provides Biblical reasons and foundations why women are called to ministry and to preach God's Word. These reasons include:

- Pentecost in which the Holy Spirit was poured out on both men and women
- In Joel 2:28, 29 it states, "[28] "And afterward, I will pour out my Spirit on all people. Your sons and daughters will prophesy, your old men will dream dreams, your young men will see visions [29] Even on my servants, both men and women, I will pour out my Spirit in those days.
- Philip had four daughters that prophesized, or preached.
- Apostle Paul called Priscilla, as well as, Aquila, his "helper" or "fellow-laborer"
- Phoebe was described as "servant of the church" in Romans 16:1
- Apostle Paul often spoke of the women that labored with him in the Gospel.
- 1 Corinthians 11 describes if a woman prophesizes how she should be adorned

It is for these reasons that Julia could not be convinced against or discouraged about her calling to preach the Gospel.

Section 81 – 84

Julia attended the conference in Philadelphia per the leading of the Holy
Spirit. It was there that she rented a meeting room and a group of women
had services with preaching and a love feast (a meal shared to demonstrate
love one for another and harmony in the faith).

Julia reminds us in these sections (81-84) that faith leads to action. 1 Peter
1:7 tells us that faith will be tried by fire. It states, " ⁷That the trial of
your faith, being much more precious than of gold that perisheth, though
it be tried with fire, might be found unto praise and honour and glory at
the appearing of Jesus Christ. (KJV)

Section 85 – 89

Julia met with her parents and was surprised when her mother commented,
"when I heard that you were a preacher, I said I would rather hear you
were dead". What a terrible shock and disappointment this comment made
on Julia. But her mother recanted that after hearing of Julia's preaching
ability, she was satisfied. This provided Julia with solace.

Julia continued to preach in churches and in homes as would be permitted.
Still the rejection met her as a woman preacher. Julia persevered in the
rejection by knowing that God would fight her battles and the weapons
He used were spiritual. Julia pressed on.

Section 90 – 93

Julia attended the General Conference of the AME Church where she was
met with harmony with few exceptions. A male attendee of the conference

offered a motion to allow women preachers to become conference members, but the motion was met with tremendous opposition. So no action was taken.

Section 94 – 98

In 1849 both Julia's husband and father met death. Julia's husband died aboard a sea vessel and her father at his home. Julia was stunned by both deaths but knew God would carry her through the sorrow with gladness to know both confessed Christ.

Her father on his deathbed exhorted Julia saying, "My dear daughter, be faithful to the heavenly calling, and fear not to preach full salvation." After time spent with family, Julia continued on her evangelistic travels.

Julia was like the apostle Paul moving from place to place over time in missionary fashion. She traveled to New York, Massachusetts, Connecticut, New Jersey, Maryland, Ohio, Pennsylvania, Michigan and Washington DC as she preached the Gospel.

Section 99 – 100

Julia survived and continued to minister although she had several exposures to slave masters seeking to interrogate her about whether she was a slave or hiding slaves.

In these sections Julia mentions that many of those called to ministry did not keep their charge and fell away from the faith, but God sustained her ministry.

Section 101 – 107

Julia in 1850 became very ill, even unto death, but she survived the vicious fever that raged within her body. She was weakened and it took some time to recover. After some level of recovery she continued preaching.

In 1851 she was asked to preach at white congregation Methodist churches, but refused unless colored people could also attend the church to hear the message. This was unheard of because of segregationist beliefs. But, Julia's refusal to preach unless coloreds could attend, led to the opening of churches to allow whites and coloreds to hear her message together.

At the encouragement of an influential community man in Detroit, Julia wrote a sermon on "A Threshing". This sermon was notable as it was taken from Isaiah (as Isaiah 21 and 23 contain threshing analogies). Julia believed that it led to the salvation of the influential man.

Section 108 – 111

In 1851 Julia traveled internationally as she visited Canada and was well received. She then returned to Ohio and took permanent residence in Cleveland, Ohio. It was there that infirmity arose as throat difficulties occurred to Julia.

Julia was convinced that the throat difficulties were a temptation to see if she would wait on the Lord for healing and guidance. She lists three reasons in which temptations surface:

- Temptations result from a corrupt nature (a sinful nature)
- Infirmity of our nature, as we live in clay tabernacles
- Temptations come from the enemy of our souls (Satan)

Julia also believed that afflictions are permitted to:

- Try of faith
- Exercise our patience
- Cause resignation to God's Will
- Ensure human dependence on God
- Teach trust in God alone

At this time Julia's mother who was suffering with feeble health came to live with her in Cleveland. Her mother died while traveling to visit Julia's sisters.

Julia mentions in this section, "The Christian Harvester" a book of living light.

The Christian Harvester:

The Christian Harvester is a publication that was founded in 1873 in Canton, Ohio by Rev. Thomas K. Doty. It was an evangelical publication that provided the tenets of the Holiness Movement.

Section 112 – 114

In these sections Julia writes a **"Letter to Christian Sisters"** that must be read rather than commented upon. It is a powerful treatise (written discourse) that provides a wealth of wisdom on the "High and Holy Call" of God.

A warning is also given to not forfeit the heavenly blessing of holiness by retreating under trials. It also provides a demand that women not get concerned about the lack of clarity of the calling, but to stick with the pursuit of the Holy Spirit to make the calling clear and plain.

Read the Foote book sections 112—114 for yourself.

Section 115 – 121
Read these sections for yourself.

Julia concludes her book with sections on "loving not the world". Julia includes a number of scriptures as if providing an apologetic discourse to love God and not the things of the world. Loving worldly things and pleasures moves you away from living a holy life that is pleasing to God.

This is a section that provides advice to women about holiness, faith, patience, perseverance human and spiritual desires, and manners of women adornment in order to be made complete in God. She encourages those called to ministry to seek the nourishment of God's Word to feed His people. Julia emphatically states, the minister's whole self must be immersed in God's holiness per the spirit, soul, and body.

Lastly, Julia exhorts that the way to obtain holiness is by faith. She states, "Faith is the only condition of sanctification." She concludes with a song, "Holy is the Lamb"; a prayer for the blessing of holiness to be given to the reader and the church; and concludes with a Doxology from Ephesians 3:20.

May the autobiography of Julia A. J. Foote richly bless you and encourage you as you seek God's purpose for your life and at times have to travel "Into the Midst of the Fire". Amen!